RADICAL FEMINISM, WRITING, AND CRITICAL AGENCY

SUNY series in Feminist Criticism and Theory

Michelle A. Massé, editor

RADICAL FEMINISM, WRITING, AND CRITICAL AGENCY

From Manifesto to Modem

~~~

Jacqueline Rhodes

State University of New York Press

Published by
State University of New York Press, Albany

© 2005 State University of New York

For information, address State University of New York Press,
90 State Street, Suite 700, Albany, NY 12207

Production by Judith Block
Marketing by Susan Petrie

Library of Congress Cataloging-in-Publication Data

Rhodes Jacqueline, 1965–
    Radical feminism, writing, and critical agency : from manifesto to modem / Jacqueline Rhodes.
        p. cm. — (SUNY series in feminist criticism and theory)
    Includes bibliographical references and index.
    ISBN 0-7914-6291-9 (alk. paper) — ISBN 0-7914-6292-7 (pbk. : alk. paper)
    1. Feminist theory. 2. Feminism. 3. Radicalism. I. Title. II. Series.

HQ1190.R53 2004
305.42—dc22   #541038 10

                                                    2004041678

10 9 8 7 6 5 4 3 2 1

For Dorothy and Merval Rhodes

CONTENTS

Contents

ACKNOWLEDGMENTS

I would like to acknowledge the support and friendship of Evelyn Ashton-Jones, whose enthusiasm for the study of rhetoric, composition, and feminism inspired my own. I would also like to thank Aurora Wolfgang and Mary Boland, who wielded their considerable reading and responding skills most graciously; James Peltz and the editorial board of SUNY Press; and the anonymous manuscript reviewers, who offered constructive suggestions for revision.

Parts of chapter 3 and chapter 4 appeared previously as "'Substantive and Feminist Girlie Action': Women Online," *College Composition and Communication* 54 (2002): 116–42 (© 2002 by the National Council of Teachers of English. Reprinted with permission.).

INTRODUCTION

In the sentence that begins her introduction to 1970's *Sisterhood is Powerful,* Robin Morgan writes that "this book is an action,"[1] a statement of textual performativity that might slide easily into many conversations in contemporary composition theory some 30 years later. Morgan's statement denotes the political significance of a text written, produced, and published by women in order to document the U.S. women's liberation movement for posterity. More importantly, Morgan's linking of textuality and liberatory action points directly to the textuality of second-wave feminism itself, particularly the movement's radical branch. Radical feminists in the late 1960s and early 1970s poured out "temporary" texts—manifestos, statements of purpose, guides to consciousness-raising and other political actions—that were often written collaboratively, distributed collectively and publicly through the magic of mimeography and volunteer effort, and that often disappeared as quickly as they had appeared in the public eye. The rhetoric of radical feminism, with its roots in the topos of political transformation, was a rhetoric of manifestos, conscious political interruptions aimed neither at assimilation nor the separate-but-equal essentializing of difference. Instead, radical feminist texts such as *The Redstockings Manifesto* and Shulamith Firestone's *The Dialectic of Sex* focused on refiguring the politics of gender, sexuality, and the family.

The particular textual subjectivity constructed by radical feminists offers a unique example of critical writing and literacy practices, an example from which many fields—most particularly rhetoric and composition studies—could learn. *Radical Feminism, Writing, and Critical Agency* seeks to answer the question of why the textual subjectivity of the radical feminist texts, both of the manifestos of the 1960s and contemporary feminist online sites, has yet to make its mark on how we think about (and teach) writing. Radical feminist textuality, with its emphasis on temporary positionality and its use of available technologies, offers much to compositionists, particularly to those seeking to revisit the issue of agency in cultural studies approaches to composition. These approaches all too often either construct the writer-agent as a site so overdetermined by cultural discourses as to preclude resistance at all, or posit the writer-agent as a *readerly* subject, one whose ability to act is constituted exclusively by textual consumption. The enactment of agency, especially temporary agency, through text and technology seems particularly relevant to us as we attempt to theorize and teach the negotiation of public and private discourses. *Radical Feminism, Writing, and Critical Agency* offers one view of a successful negotiation by contextualizing radical feminist manifestos of the 1960s and 1970s and feminist Web sites of today within the history of composition studies. However separated these texts may be by 30 years of theoretical and technological change, an exploration of their interconnections can offer us insight into the workings of positionality, literacy, and technology.

As new classroom and textual structures become more common in writing instruction, it seems imperative that we look to the particular literacies developed in response to those structures. More importantly, we must look to these literacies as collective responses designed to work social change. Lester Faigley, in his 1996 CCCC Chair's address, noted that the Enlightenment's nobler values—civic virtue, just community, and social equality—were

> developed and spread primarily through the practices of literacy. We know that literacy education has often not lived up to these ideals and has functioned instead to label individuals and groups as deficient, inferior, and unworthy. Nevertheless, these ideals have provided the means of critique for educational practices that uphold illegitimate hierarchies of power.[2]

It is my belief that the radical feminist manifestos of the 1960s and certain feminist Web sites today bespeak a textual subjectivity formed for the (almost explicit) critique of "illegitimate hierarchies of power." The fluid textuality of the radical feminists provides us with a view of what Susan Miller has termed the "textual subject," a subject who temporarily yet purposefully *acts*—and acts through writing.

If we believe that composition at its best can encourage students to think, read, and write critically—and if we believe that feminist approaches to composition are a key part of that project—then we need to reexamine the conversation about feminism and writing, particularly that conversational gap that is radical feminism. We need to rethink our histories of composition studies and feminism to examine how the overtly agonistic discourse of the women's *liberation* movement has been silenced in favor of the more contained discourse of the women's *rights* movement.[3] We need, as well, to open wide the ideological rifts between feminist and cultural studies approaches to composition, if for no other reason than to develop our own critical consciousness about who, precisely, it is we want to liberate in our classrooms. That is, we need to explore more fully the disjuncture between what Miller calls the "theory we say we have" about writing and the "theory we actually have" about writing, as evidenced by our teaching practices.[4] It is my intention in this work to provide one such exploration.

At the core of this study is the idea that it is crucial for feminists and composition scholars to identify, historicize, and articulate the intentionally resistant discourses of radical feminism. Such an articulation not only offers an examination of feminist rhetoric in itself, answering Lynn Worsham's recent call to "consciously narrate" the history of feminism,[5] but also situates the writer as a rhetorical agent whose positionality is not limited to the idea of the writer-as-reader. Perhaps even more importantly, an articulation of transgressive discourses positions the writer-agent as neither a univocal "author" nor a passive intersection of the discourses of power. Rather, it can position the writer-agent as Miller's textual subject, a subject who consciously fictionalizes stability in order to write, to resist, and to act. It is my hope that such a conception of the "subject" of writing will contribute to other current efforts in rhetoric and composition studies to retheorize student writers as active producers of the strategic discourses of resistance.

1

FEMINISM, COMPOSITION, AND RE-HISTORY

BUILDING FEMINIST COMMUNITY within composition has as one of its projects the historicization of women within rhetoric and composition, historicization that includes critical work such as Cheryl Glenn's *Rhetoric Retold* and Jacqueline Jones Royster's *Traces in a Stream*,[1] as well as self-reflexive narratives of attempts to negotiate composition studies as a feminist, as in Elizabeth Flynn's serial commentary on her own 1988 "Composing as a Woman." As Suzanne Clark notes, Flynn's ongoing work "exemplifies the way much feminist work mobilizes the uncertainty produced by historical change."[2] The act of historicization within feminist composition studies is crucial to the formation of a site from which to speak as a feminist. Although it constitutes only one strand of conversation in contemporary composition studies regarding feminism, historicization ties intimately to each of the other strands: its projects play a key part in discussions of the status of women in the field; in the discussions of research methods that led to the work of Carol Gilligan and Mary Field Belenky (and thus to the work of many cultural feminists in composition); and, to a lesser extent, in discussions of postmodern and cultural studies approaches to composition.

This last connection is the most problematic, perhaps because of how the other connections have formed and been deployed in composition studies. That is, because of a relatively uncritical approach to the history of the intersections of feminism and composition studies, it is difficult if not impossible to reconcile postmodern conceptions of agency with the discourse of empowerment so often present in discussions of feminist pedagogy. This uncritical approach to history is surprising, given the critical historicization that has led to such diverse work as Clark's examination of the "despised rhetoric" of sentimentality, Joann Campbell's revaluation of Gertrude Buck, and Susan Miller's commentary on the material conditions of women within composition studies.[3] Discussions of postmodern and poststructuralist feminism within composition most often have to do with the French feminists, as in the work of Lynn Worsham and Clara Juncker.[4] While feminist compositionists have used different post-theories to good advantage in discussions of materiality and the incommensurability of theory, they do not juxtapose those two impulses. That is, feminists do not bring the tools of critical historicist analysis to bear on their own history; they do not look at their own historicist texts.

As feminists themselves have pointed out, uncritical histories too often present an "objective" god's-eye view dependent on elision for its coherence; in short, what does not fit the narrative is left out or ignored. An uncritical history of feminism in composition studies has served to contain and neutralize one of the key generative moments of public feminist discourse: the in-your-face textuality of the late-1960s radical feminists. This chapter, then, questions the historicization efforts of feminists in composition, looking to Michel Foucault's notion of genealogical history to reconfigure radical feminism's place (or lack thereof) in histories of feminism and composition. Beginning with a brief overview of Foucault's genealogical approach, I will examine the recent upsurge in interest in the historical intersections of composition and feminism; I will also explore the curious absence of radical feminism at these intersections, an absence that serves as the focal point for my study. To this end, I examine key works in this conversation, beginning with Caywood and Overing's 1987 *Teaching Writing: Pedagogy, Gender, and Equity* and Flynn's 1988 article, continuing through scattered articles by Miller, Susan Jarratt, Worsham, and others, and coming to the present with the collections edited by Louise Wetherbee Phelps and Janet Emig *(Feminine Principles)* and Jarratt and Worsham *(In Other Words)*.

FOUCAULT, FEMINISM, AND GENEALOGY

Foucault's work has been a highly productive yet contested site for feminist theorists; even as they might acknowledge Foucault's importance to the development of critical insights about power and subjectivity, feminists find Foucault's gender blindness and his negation of agency problematic. Nancy Hartsock points out that postmodern theory in general does not allow for emancipatory action, a particular sticking-point for a movement such as feminism, which has as one defining feature its emphasis on liberatory action. Hartsock writes that "for those of us who have been marginalized and subjugated in various ways and who need to understand the world systematically in order to change it, postmodernist theories at their best fail to provide an alternative to the Enlightenment."[5] In a similar vein, Sabina Lovibond questions the will to postmodernity, asking "How can anyone ask me to say goodbye to 'emancipatory metanarratives' when my own emancipation is still such a patchy, hit-and-miss affair?"[6] Many feminist critics find it suspicious that the idea of "agency" dies out in critical thought just at the time when hitherto "unauthorized" people have a chance to wield some sort of author-ity.

It is thus that Foucault's *Discipline and Punish* and *The History of Sexuality*, with their reconceptualization of power and subjectivity, hold tenuous and somewhat contradictory positions in feminist studies. On the one hand, Foucault's argument that power inscribes, saturates, and even constitutes every human relation ties closely to feminist critiques of language and culture. On the other hand, that argument specifically challenges the very idea of emancipatory politics and individual or collective agency. That is, as in the feminist critique of postmodern theories in general, the feminist critique of Foucault reflects the seeming ideological impossibility of advocating social and political change while using a theoretical framework that denies the possibility of changing exploitative power relations.

Hartsock writes that Foucault's claim that we are all, regardless of gender, race, class, age, or sexual orientation, implicated in the deployment of unequal power relations ultimately leads to critical paralysis. That is, she argues, by following Foucault's insistence on metaphors of webs and nets of power (instead of structures of domination), "we are led to conclude merely that each of us both dominates and is dominated. We are all responsible, and so in a sense no one is responsible. Thus, the question of how to analyze structures of domination is obscured."[7] In short, if power saturates every relation, there is no place outside power from which to resist. At the same time, Foucault implies that there is no real possibility of radical resistance inside the web of power relations; at best, we can only reform the conditions under which our bodies are made docile. As Monique Deveaux writes, "Foucault's extreme reluctance to attribute specific agency to subjects in his early accounts of power results in a portrayal of individuals as passive bodies, constituted by power and immobilized in a society of discipline."[8]

Even writers who ultimately reject the use of Foucault for feminism, however, acknowledge that his ideas have influenced contemporary feminist theory greatly. In composition, Foucaultian ideas have shaped material analyses of subjects such as classroom layout and freshman composition programs. In *Working Theory,* Judith Goleman uses the work of Mikhail Bakhtin and Louis Althusser to show the liminal space of practice/theory as a site for textual agency; underneath her "direct dialogues" with these theorists, however, she relies upon Foucault's analysis of the relations of power, knowledge, and discourse to orient her project.[9] In "On the Subjects of Class and Gender in 'The Literacy Letters'" (1989), Linda Brodkey uses an exchange of letters between graduate student teachers of basic writing and ABE (Adult Basic Education) students to explore the possibility of discursive resistance within a Foucaultian framework. My purpose in offering these examples of productive use of Foucault's work is not to rehabilitate that work for feminists, or to suggest that feminist concerns about the work are unfounded. Rather, it is to note that certain insoluble tensions exist in such use and that it is crucial that we acknowledge the tensions without rejecting certain productive possibilities offered through Foucault.

For the purposes of my own project, I draw from Foucault's revisioning of history, a revision produced through a genealogical approach to the past. While Enlightenment thought positions history as a coherent trajectory supported by a metaphysical belief in "truth," Foucault presents a genealogical model of history that "points to the inequality of forces as the source of values or the work of ressentiment in the production of the objective world."[10] The philosophy of history (against which Foucault posits his genealogical method) depends on a cause-effect view of historical events and on the idea of some metaphysical origin from which we came and to which we go. That is, as Foucault writes in "Theatrum Philosophicum," the philosophy of history:

> encloses the event in a cyclical pattern of time. Its error is grammatical; it treats the present as framed by the past and future: the present is a former future where its form was prepared and the past, which will occur in the future, preserves the identity of its content. First, this sense of the present requires a logic of essences (which establishes the present in memory) and of concepts (where the present is established as a knowledge of the future), and then a metaphysics of a crowned and coherent cosmos, of a hierarchical world.[11]

I quote this passage at some length because it contains several key points for any critical examination of the intersection of feminism, composition, and history. First, teleological history offers no way to account for singularity—present events happen because of a past condition, past events happened because of a prior condition. What does not fit in that coherent causal whole is a curiosity, not part of history; in fact, as in the case of radical feminism in the history of composition studies, it may be invisible. Genealogies, in contrast, are elucidations of anomaly, narratives that do not "neglect the vicissitudes of history."[12] Second, the dependence on the logic of essence and concept informs much of the feminist conversation in composition. Finally, while it is an overstatement to claim that feminists in composition always rely on a metaphysics of hierarchy to frame their own arguments, it is certainly true that the metaphysics of hierarchy almost always play a part in any liberatory movement. Feminism is no exception; like the issues of individual agency and emancipatory action, the metaphysics of hierarchy serve as a site of much contention in feminist discussion of Foucault.

The main advantage to a Foucaultian approach to history is that it acknowledges the rhetoricity of historicization itself. The choices that any history makes about singularity, essence, and the metaphysics of hierarchy are rhetorical choices, invested heavily in questions of who writes the histories, who reads them, and the purposes for which the writing and reading are done. Feminists in composition have written their history in specific ways to accomplish specific ends; indeed, one reason that radical feminism disappears from current discussions of feminism and composition studies is that 1960s feminisms are often collapsed into a manageable

whole on our way to the work of Carol Gilligan and the Belenky collaborative.[13] My statement is by no means an indictment of compositionists
in particular; indeed, as Alice Echols demonstrates in her *Daring to Be
Bad*, radical feminism dissipated into a more general, shorthand "feminism" in part because of its own theoretical limitations, its problematic
universalism, and its status *as* radical—that is, as Echols writes, it suffered
"the fate of all social change movements."[14]

I would contend, however, that the affinity of the work of Gilligan
and the Belenky collaborative with cultural feminism *necessarily* contributes to the absence of radical feminism in discussions of composition. It is difficult to overstate the influence of these works in feminist
developmental psychology on feminist composition studies. Gilligan's
In a Different Voice: Psychological Theory and Women's Development
(1982) challenged then-prevailing assumptions about moral development, positing that women's moral development was substantially different from men's; and the Belenky collaborative's *Women's Ways of
Knowing: The Development of Self, Voice, and Mind* (1986), explored the
ways in which "gender influences knowing and learning."[15] The idea of
"women's different ways" forms a crucial connection between feminist
developmental psychology and cultural feminist rhetoric as it appears
in contemporary rhetoric and composition scholarship; this connection, in turn, contributes to a loss of a sense of critical agency in writing classrooms, through the reification of the ideas of teacher-as-
mother, writing-as-expression, and classroom-as-nurturing space.

THE METAPHYSICS OF "WOMEN'S WAYS" OF WRITING

It is not my intent to provide a comprehensive overview of feminism
and composition studies, but instead to examine, specifically, how these
two fields have defined "feminism" and "women" in the context of writing instruction. These definitions have served to perpetuate a cultural
feminist ideology in feminist composition studies, an ideology that
serves as the justifying narrative behind the radical-free history of feminism and composition. When radical feminism *does* appear in histories of feminism and composition, it is often reduced to a mishistoricized tale of consciousness-raising groups and a problematic tendency
to universalize. This construction of radical feminism serves a twofold
purpose: it effectively removes radical feminism from real critique,

since our misapprehension creates a "straw feminist," as it were, and it keeps us from obtaining those insights we might otherwise gain from radical feminist textuality.

Some reexamination of earlier texts is necessary to demonstrate the extent to which feminist composition studies depends upon humanist assumptions about individual agency and about history. In effect, I will sketch out the ways in which feminist composition studies has relied on a teleological, cyclical pattern of time in order to present the "coherent cosmos" of our discipline. My purpose in this section, therefore, is twofold. First, I wish to examine the particular ways in which these texts have served to present "feminism" to the larger composition community; feminism in these texts is cultural feminism, marked by its valorization of "women's ways," and in composition marked by a "happy marriage" to expressivist thought.[16] Second, I wish to show how this valorization continues to shape feminist thought in composition, most notably in Phelps and Emig's recent collection, *Feminine Principles and Women's Experience in American Composition and Rhetoric*. Many of the collection's individual authors do not position themselves as cultural feminists: Evelyn Ashton-Jones's gender critique of collaborative learning and Patricia Bizzell's historicist "Praising Folly: Constructing a Postmodern Rhetorical Authority as a Woman," for example, both focus on positionality within discourses of power rather than on revaluing an undervalued "female nature." However, the editors of the collection make it clear that *they* have framed their collection according to cultural feminist values. Phelps and Emig write that their feminism "depended powerfully on constantly negotiating" the "dynamic tension [of] the complementary principles defined in our culture as feminine and masculine."[17] Their vision of their collection, if not the collection itself, participates in the creation of a coherent, causally oriented march through composition's history that seems to be the focus of feminist historicization projects, and to a lesser extent the focus of attempts to incorporate feminist pedagogy into the composition classroom.

According to cultural feminists in composition, "women's ways" and "feminine principles," coherent through the time and space of decades of composition pedagogy, have been systematically ignored. That is, as Eileen E. Schell writes:

> cultural feminists argue that feminine values have been denigrated and superseded by masculine values such as aggressiveness, confrontation,

control, competition, domination, and physical violence. To reverse the perpetuation of harmful masculine values, cultural feminists contend that all people—men and women alike—should emulate feminine values: nurturance, supportiveness, interdependence, and nondominance.[18]

A generous interpretation of this stance would note that cultural feminists in composition draw from Gayatri Spivak, that is, they argue that to reclaim women's ways for the field requires a "strategic essentialism" designed to subvert the patriarchal, hierarchical principles of current-traditional rhetoric. However, because this essentialism depends on present-tense woman framed by past and future women with historically coherent "ways of being," it serves more to *perpetuate* the "crowned and coherent cosmos" than to *subvert* it. Rather than positing essentialism as a temporary and rhetorically bound strategy, feminist histories of rhetoric and composition neglect "the vicissitudes of history," as Foucault might say.[19] In other words, these histories neglect the curiosities, the anomalies, and the singular parts that do not "fit" into the ahistorical, a-rhetorical cosmos of cultural feminist composition.

The problematic contemporary conversation about the intersections of feminism and composition studies, as most scholars would attest, opens with two texts: 1987's *Teaching Writing: Pedagogy, Gender, and Equity,* a collection edited by Cynthia L. Caywood and Gillian R. Overing, and Flynn's 1988 "Composing as a Woman." Both texts draw heavily from the work of Nancy Chodorow, Carol Gilligan, and the group of scholars who collaborated on *Women's Ways of Knowing* (Mary Field Belenky, Blythe McVicker Clinchy, Nancy Rule Goldberger, and Jill Mattuck Tarule). Each of these texts, in turn, relies upon a logic of essence and concept to expand the borders of (but not radically change) the humanist subject. As Laura Brady notes in "The Reproduction of Othering," the synecdochal use of experience as evidence in Chodorow's *The Reproduction of Mothering,* Gilligan's *In a Different Voice,* and *Women's Ways of Knowing* makes use of a strategic essentialism. In all three texts, Brady writes, "individual narratives became the basis for generalizations about the collective identity of woman"; she further argues that repeated citation of these works has "institutionalized a popular concept of the category of woman, which has helped create a newly established set of gender conventions that both feminists and antifeminists appropriate."[20]

Brady uses Michel de Certeau's distinction between strategies and tactics, pointing out that feminism as both an "institution" and a "counterinstitutional movement" works strategically and tactically. As tactics become visible and bear repetition, they become strategies; thus, Brady argues, "the work of Chodorow, Gilligan, and the Belenky collaborative continues to have a strategic value but that it has lost much of its interventionary (tactical) use for contemporary feminist composition theory."[21] Like the work of Chodorow, Gilligan, and the Belenky collaborative, *Teaching Writing* and "Composing as a Woman" makes the move from tactical to strategic value through repeated citation. In addition, they write a history that insists that the category of woman not only exists in a particular way, but that it has always existed in that way. "Woman" as described in the work of Chodorow, Gilligan, and the Belenky collaborative becomes naturalized through its encounters with feminist compositionists.

Caywood and Overing's *Teaching Writing* makes a book-length claim, spanning each of the articles within the volume, that process-oriented collaborative pedagogy and feminist goals are closely related. Schell writes that in the book, "female students' subjectivities are represented as buried treasure, which must be brought to light with the assistance of the feminist teacher."[22] The collection's claim, then, relies on an uncritical acceptance of the idea of an individual voice and an authentic self that can be articulated in writing; given the appropriate (feminist or process) pedagogy, writing classrooms can change not only how one writes but who one is when one writes. Overall, contributors to *Teaching Writing* suggest that feminist classrooms can counteract patriarchal pedagogy's "emphasis on hierarchy, competition, and control."[23] In their introduction to the collection, for example, Caywood and Overing write that the key relation between feminism and composition is "the relation between revisionist critiques of traditional writing theory and the feminist critique of masculinist, patriarchal ways of being."[24] Further, they write that "the process model, insofar as it facilitates and legitimizes the fullest expression of the individual voice, is compatible with the feminist revisioning of hierarchy, if not essential to it."[25] In their own contribution to the book, "Writing Across the Curriculum: a Model for a Workshop and a Call for Change," they write that process pedagogy abandons the ideas of "authority" and "model" in favor of "facilitator" and "process," a change that creates a "less-structured, less rigidly hierarchical, revalued, collaborative, open-ended approach" that "is compatible with feminism, if not feminist in and of itself."[26]

Caywood and Overing's claim that feminist (and process) pedagogy can facilitate the development of the individual woman's voice—which is and has always been (essentially) the voice of a noncompetitive, maternal-thinking nurturer—forms a key component of almost every essay in the collection. In "Women Writing," for example, Wendy Goulston writes that traditional (non-process) writing pedagogies prevent women students from writing authentically, since "the woman who excels at school learns to write pleasing papers for professors, [but] she does not write them from her whole 'center.'"[27] Similarly, Rebecca Blevins Faery's "Women and Writing Across the Curriculum: Learning and Liberation" explores how the process model of writing makes students more active learners, which is "particularly important for women students, to help them overcome the tendencies toward passivity and intellectual dependence and timidity which are their cultural heritage."[28] In her contribution to the anthology, Carol A. Stanger writes that collaborative learning is a feminist pedagogy in that it "taps learners' early experience with their mothers."[29] Elisabeth Däumer and Sandra Runzo examine the "maternal perspective" in Janet Emig's work and valorize a "maternal teacher" who "attempts to meet students on their own grounds, to individualize instruction, and to allow for self-sponsored writing by encouraging students to interact as much with each other as with the instructor."[30] While Däumer and Runzo note that "mothering" has not been adequately critiqued, particularly the role of the mother as enforcer of traditional femininity, their essay spends a good deal of time recuperating "maternal teaching" as that which more adequately addresses the needs of women's voices, both as teachers and students.[31]

Like Caywood and Overing's collection, Flynn's "Composing as a Woman" valorizes maternal teaching and emphasizes the newly feminized humanist subject as justified by a logic of essence. Flynn claims that "composition specialists replace the figure of the authoritative father with an image of a nurturing mother"[32] and suggests that women and men write differently because of their different experiences with their mothers. Further, like the essays in *Teaching Writing*, Flynn's early work presents a feminism grounded in the work of Chodorow, Gilligan, and the Belenky collaborative, all of which she claims is "especially relevant to a feminist consideration of student writing."[33] She writes that scholars should not assume that "males and females use language in identical ways or represent the world in a similar fashion. And if their writing strategies and patterns of representation do differ, then ignoring those differences almost certainly means a suppression of women's separate ways of thinking and writing."[34] It is important to note that Flynn distances herself (in a later article) from the claim that process pedagogy and feminist pedagogy are necessarily synonymous. As Clark writes in response to several articles citing Flynn in 1998's *Feminism and Composition Studies: In Other Words:*

> the difference between the Flynn of "Composing as a Woman" and the Flynn of the 1995 review illustrates the danger of taking woman out of history, text out of context. It illustrates the danger of losing sight of the rhetorical situation. Abandoning the rhetorical approach is fatal, since that approach is the best contribution to feminism that women in composition can make.[35]

"Composing as a Woman," along with Flynn's later work, addresses a serious inattention to the intersections of gender and discourse in composition studies, a phenomenon that Flynn herself points to when she writes that at the time of the article, "the fields of feminist studies and composition studies have not engaged each other in a serious or systematic way."[36] Well over a decade later, Flynn's assessment still holds true, but equally lasting is her contribution to the problematic historicization of feminism in composition studies. Her early article, drawing its energy from the reinscription and naturalization of gender roles (essence) and an elision of difference in favor of universalized woman, makes the history of feminism and composition coherent, causal, dependent on an origin of grace (gender-balanced pedagogy) from which we have fallen.

More importantly, the nurturing, maternal-thinking woman constructed as "natural" in texts such as "Composing as a Woman," *Teaching Writing,* and others appears as the inevitable outcome of feminist history, a metaphysical copy of the "original" woman whose presence in the past ensures, through the causal coherence of teleological history, her presence in the present. That is, the ways in which feminist compositionists tell the history of feminism in composition creates a *particular* feminism and a *particular* composition, both of which depend on their prior justification to explain their current situation. What cannot be accounted for in those histories is rendered unnatural, perverse, or invisible. A particular aporia in this history is radical feminism which, if it is alluded to at all, is presented uncritically. In "Silences: Feminist Language Research and the Teaching of Writing," for example, Pamela J. Annas offers a short history of the intersections of contemporary feminism and writing in order to create a past that frames the present as something inevitable and thus natural. Annas's particular interest in the radical feminists is their commitment to consciousness-raising. Beginning with the works of Betty Friedan and Tillie Olsen, Annas moves to a discussion of late 1960s consciousness-raising groups, in which (according to Annas) women talked, listened, and then found "common threads" in their own stories and other women's. Annas writes that the key discursive development here was "a form of discourse . . . based on cooperation and augmentation rather than competitiveness, on dialogue rather than hierarchy."[37] Similarly, in a 1990 article, Joy Ritchie cautions against "a return to naïve consciousness-raising groups," which she sets in opposition to a desire for "historical, critical analysis and, thus, for action."[38]

Consciousness-raising is not the only trace left of the radical feminists; feminist compositionists occasionally invoke radical feminism in order to dissociate themselves from its synecdochal, difference-erasing view of women's experience, that is, the belief in women's "sisterhood." Harriet Malinowitz, for example, in her 1998 "A Feminist Critique of Writing in the Disciplines," claims that the "early second wave of feminism based much of its thinking" on the belief that local knowledge is unitary, "and feminism has been reeling and learning from that mistake ever since."[39] She writes that much second-wave feminist writing "held that the category of women signaled not only a collective of bodies bound together by the fact of their common oppression but also an epistemological location—that is, it constituted a site of local knowledge (in the spiritual or experiential, not geographical, sense)."[40] Feminist composition scholarship is peppered with such quick, uncritical characterizations of the radical feminist movement and its discursive tactics, leaving in question the extent to which those characterizations are true and to what ends these tactics were employed. In the specific case of consciousness-raising, these quick takes construct a self-justifying past, a shorthand depiction of second-wave feminism that ignores both the public-directed ends of consciousness-raising groups and the extremely contentious discussions of the purpose and consciousness-raising that took place at the time the groups existed. That is, a common concern about consciousness-raising groups was that they existed only to provide a space for self-actualization for white, middle-class women. However, radical feminists saw consciousness-raising as only a first step toward liberation; the necessary second step was putting that newly raised consciousness into direct protest and often agonistic public action. In "Catching the Fire," for example, former Redstocking Rosalyn Fraad Baxandall writes that her group's consciousness-raising sessions often led to direct political protest. "Armed with our critique of marriage," she writes of one instance, "we decided to invade [with WITCH] a commercial bridal fair at Madison Square Garden. Our flyer said 'Confront the Whoremakers'"[41]

Not all feminist compositionists present the uncritical, shorthand view of radical feminism so prevalent in the field. Jarratt, for example, in her introduction to *Feminism and Composition Studies: In Other Words*, writes that in the late 1960s and early 1970s, consciousness-raising groups provided a space in which women not only "told their stories," but "made the personal political";[42] this move from personal revelation to public and political action was the raison d'être of consciousness-raising groups, at least according to the radical feminists. Jarratt does address the universalizing pull of radical feminist theory, writing that "as the metaphor of sisterhood reached the limits of its usefulness as a political gathering place for feminists in the second wave, this figure began to obscure more than it revealed, hiding differences under wraps, suggesting that all women had common experiences, goals, and languages."[43] Worsham offers a slightly different take on "sisterhood" in her "After Words" in the same volume, noting that second-wave feminists understood the metaphor of sisterhood "as a symbol of unity that encompassed all women and still acknowledged their diversity."[44]

It is important to note that Jarratt, Worsham, and other feminists have problematized the conversation about feminism and writing pedagogy almost from the time that the conversation began. Indeed, the discussions of feminism and composition have never presented unitary visions of a happy convergence of process pedagogy and women in the classroom. *Teaching Writing* and "Composing as a Woman" appeared only a short time before more constructivist approaches to feminism appeared in composition studies, most notably a special issue of *JAC: Journal of Advanced Composition* focusing on gender, culture, and ideology in 1990, and 1991's *Contending with Words: Composition and Rhetoric in a Postmodern Age*, which contains both Jarratt's "Feminism and Composition: The Case for Conflict" and Worsham's "Writing against Writing: The Predicament of *Ecriture Féminine* in Composition Studies." In the special issue of *JAC*, guest-edited by Ashton-Jones, articles range from a Ritchie's critique of essentialist thinking in feminist pedagogy (containing as it does the previous unfortunate quick reference to consciousness-raising) to Mary Kupiec Cayton's exploration of women's writing blocks. Like the authors in *Teaching Writing*, the authors in *JAC* 10.2 draw some theoretical energy from the work of Gilligan and the Belenky collaborative; however, they do not use that energy to posit a coherent, naturalized narrative of women in composition. In "No Exit: A Play of Literacy and Gender," for example, Don Kraemer writes warily of the cultural feminist drive to valorize "women's ways," noting that

> Polarities like symbolic activity versus synecdochic activity, male language versus female language, game world versus nongame world—these distinctions may be necessary and productive of discourse, but they are not foundational. They don't stay in place or guarantee our politics. It is perhaps inevitable but surely mistaken to assign permanent plus and minus values to such distinctions . . .[45]

Likewise, Wendy Bishop, in "Learning Our Own Ways to Situate Composition and Feminist Studies in the English Department," mentions *Women's Ways of Knowing* as just one of several possible approaches to rethinking how feminist compositionists mentor graduate students.

Jarratt, in her essay in *Contending with Words*, is similarly cautious about women's ways and feminine principles. Jarratt writes that the "powerful potential" of the connections between composition and feminism remains only potential as long as we "decline to contend with words."[46] That is, she writes that viewing and teaching agonistic discourse solely as the realm of the masculine leaves students "unsufficiently [*sic*] prepared to negotiate the oppressive discourses of racism, sexism, and classism surfacing in the composition classroom" because teachers "spend too little time helping their students learn how to argue about public issues—making the turn from the personal back out to the public."[47] Worsham's essay in the same volume questions the "will to pedagogy," or the impulse to domesticate theory through seeing it only "as a source for new textual and pedagogical models and strategies."[48] Specifically, Worsham's argument should give pause to feminist compositionists looking to French feminism as a justification for teaching women's ways in the writing classroom.

In the late 1990s, the appearance of Phelps and Emig's *Feminine Principles and Women's Experience* collection and Jarratt and Worsham's *Feminism and Composition Studies* collection—two volumes with very different editorial frameworks, to be sure—illustrates the ongoing tension between feminist compositionists about how to define, theorize, and teach writing. The Phelps and Emig collection, as the editors almost explicitly point out, descends from the late 1980s work of Caywood, Overing, and Flynn. Phelps and Emig justify their use of "feminine" in the book's title (instead of "feminist") by claiming that "feminine" is the underlying, original term. "In fact," they write, "much of what is called, in our volume and elsewhere *feminist* seems to us to be claims and disclaimers about the contested feminine—women's different ways of knowing, writing, teaching, learning, and so on."[49] Whether the articles in the collection adhere to that vision is another matter; the volume begins, for example, with Ashton-Jones's critique of the uncritical view of collaborative learning that allows feminists to draw parallels between it and feminist pedagogy. Ashton-Jones writes that it "takes a logical leap of questionable validity to conclude that removing the teacher-authority from the scene of meaning making effectively removes all traces of the patriarchal presence."[50] Further, she argues, even if one assumes that collaborative learning parallels feminist discourse, "it remains to be seen whether men and women function on equal terms within the province of the group itself."[51] However, other essays in the collection, most notably Janice Hays's "Intellectual Parenting and a Developmental Feminist Pedagogy of Writing" obviously make use of the theoretical constructs valued by the collections' editors.

Jarratt and Worsham's *Feminism and Composition: In Other Words* contributes more than its editors' introduction and afterwards to the critique of cultural feminist pedagogy. In "Riding Long Coattails, Subverting Tradition: The Tricky Business of Feminists Teaching Rhetoric(s)," Joy Ritchie and Kate Ronald reexamine two recent courses that they taught to explore what it means to teach rhetoric as a feminist. Each of the courses examined rhetorical history, in both its exclusive canonical form and in its interruptions, interruptions offered by feminist recovery projects. Ritchie and Ronald write that one tension in recovery work is that too often, the search for women's texts includes an essentialist search for a woman's voice. That is, they write, readings in women's rhetoric "had to be recovered in order to redress their absence, but resisted so that students would not define women's writing as a unified, seamless whole tied to an essential female body."[52] However, they also warn that we must "recognize that recovery is often necessarily accompanied by an essentialist celebration of women's rhetoric."[53] Specifically, just as one of their editors had argued years earlier, Ritchie and Ronald worry that dividing rhetorical strategies into masculine and feminine modes both denies women's use of agonistic discourse through history and limits their abilities to intervene today. That is, they write, such division "not only may be inaccurate but also may limit women's rhetorical options and ignore the rhetorical power of much of women's writing throughout history."[54] Similarly, Schell's essay in the Jarratt/Worsham collection reexamines "femininism," a neologism created by Flynn to describe the "conscious awareness of women's special perspectives and problems and the commitment to gender equity."[55] Placing "femininism" in the context of Nel Noddings's ethics of care, Schell argues that the approach, "although compelling, may reinforce rather than critique or transform patriarchal structures."[56]

It is thus that the current conversations about feminism and composition continue. The Phelps and Emig collection and the Jarratt and Worsham collection appear to have descended separately from the same history, a history that depends less on the question of whether one engages in strategic essentialism than on the inevitability of women writing now, in this way, because of how compositionists think women wrote before. In short, this history repeats the "grammatical error" noted by Foucault: it relies on a "logic of essences," a "logic of concept," and, finally, "a metaphysics of a crowned and coherent cosmos" in order to legitimate itself *as* history.[57]

Because of the drive to legitimize ourselves within academe, and because, perhaps, we have thrown in our lot with academic feminism rather than "street" feminism, we have remained curiously silent on the subject of the public textuality of second-wave feminism. It is thus heartening to note that many compositionists have begun feminist material critiques of the field, searching something beyond metaphysics both inside the classroom and out of it. Schell's essay exists as one such critique; in it, she argues that emphasizing an ethics of care, as many cultural feminists do, "may prevent feminists from addressing one of the most serious gender problems we face in composition studies: the relegating of women to contingent (part-time and non-tenure-track) writing instructorships."[58] Citing Miller's "Feminization of Composition," Schell urges feminist compositionists to pay attention to how "institutional scripts cast women teachers as nurturers . . . thus making it problematic for feminists to continue advocating nurturant behavior as a form of empowerment."[59]

Both *Feminine Principles* and *Feminism and Composition Studies* contain discussions of the material conditions of women teaching, a conversation begun by Miller over a decade ago in her *Textual Carnivals*, in which she described the situation of composition as the "sad woman in the basement," and continued in "The Feminization of Composition" and other work. Other writers such as Flynn and Sharon Crowley have taken up the discussion, creating such a significant thread in the conversation about feminism and composition that Phelps refers to the concept of the feminization of composition as a "truism." In her own contribution to the *Feminine Principles* collection, Phelps explores the implications of being a female administrator, acknowledging that composition is "a field dominated in numbers by women, concerned with a subject and a teaching practice perceived by many academics and the public as low-status, elementary, service-oriented, menial 'women's work.'"[60]

While the current material critiques of composition certainly form an important part of the conversation about feminism and composition, they are not enough in themselves to help us escape the clutches of a history that, in valorizing "women's ways," ignores or misrepresents women's *different* ways. The singularity of the radical feminist movement, with its commitment to direct, textual, and often agonistic action, does not exist as part of the coherent narrative of feminism and composition, in which consciousness-raising groups led to our collaborative pedagogy and false universalization led to our enlightenment. Radical feminism does not contribute to the causal relation demanded by the teleological histories of feminism and composition; radical feminism, unless it is mis-historicized, cannot prejustify the present condition of the feminist writing classroom. And thus we are left to reinvent the feminist wheel; many of the debates over essentialism, diversity, and "feminine principles" that we find in contemporary scholarship appeared in print 30 years ago. In the late 1960s, as Rachel Blau Du-Plessis and Ann Snitow write, critiques of "gender-as-monocause and sisterhood-as-monocure came immediately from many locations."[61] To what do we owe our historical blind spot, if not to the need to justify our present in terms of our created past?

PRESENT TENSE: WHAT'S STILL MISSING

Certainly, feminism and composition encompasses more textual terrain than the handful of books and articles I have examined here; my point in such an examination, however, is not to produce an exhaustive history, but instead to produce a *telling* history, one that gives us its narrative through its repeated citation of the tropes of the natural, maternal-thinking woman and the nurturing, expressivist-oriented collaborative classroom that grew out of a neutralized radical feminist movement. While we may have started to engage feminism in what Flynn might call a "serious way," there is much of the engagement left unfinished. Currently, the questions about feminism in composition have to do with how women write. Do they write differently from men? What are the conditions of women teaching? Is there a women's language? What is a women's rhetoric? What women rhetoricians should we add to the history of rhetoric? The questions that we have not yet asked or answered are questions of textuality: to what political movements have women contributed? What texts did they produce, for what purpose? What were the conditions of political textual action? In short, we do not look enough outside the limits of our composition-bound history.

For contemporary feminist compositionists, it appears that radical second-wave feminism consists of consciousness-raising and a problematic tendency to universalize personal experience; in each case, radical feminism, in all its complication and division, exists only insofar as it justifies the present-tense of feminism and composition. The history that we tell becomes the present that we value, and the present that we tell becomes the history that we value. That is, either the radical feminists' consciousness-raising groups provide the utopian model for the feminist collaborative classroom, or their shortsighted universalizing tendencies are what we, having made "progress" in our feminist thought, now work against. In either case, the radical feminists are mishistoricized, dismissed too quickly as middle-class, consciousness-raising, essentializing white women, a construction that only touches the surface of the radical feminist movement and that does not address at all the unique textual and discursive action that was part and parcel of the movement. It is not my intent to dismiss the criticisms of radical feminism or to hold the radical feminists up as the "true" or "original" feminists to our own pale imitations. Rather, it is to note radical feminism as an anomaly, a phantasm that exceeds the limitations of its history as told by many contemporary feminist compositionists. What we include in our histories are the places where radical feminism "touches down" on those histories' grammatical error—where it reinforces the argument *we already want to make* about collaborative pedagogy, or women's ways, or difference.

2

REWRITING RADICAL WOMEN

IT SHOULD NOT SURPRISE feminist scholars that radical feminist texts are often difficult to locate and that they have received insufficient critical attention. Indeed, much feminist scholarship in the last 30 years has been devoted to bringing similarly neglected texts to the critical fore. Curiously, however, the texts of the radical feminist movement form a gap in such recovery efforts. Although some of the radical feminists' work has survived in anthologies such as Morgan's, in special collections such as those at the University of Michigan and Duke University, in women's libraries at campus women's centers, and in cardboard boxes and attics, much of it has been out of print since the mid-1970s. After the work served its most obvious rhetorical purpose—making feminism a visible, textual, *manifest* presence in public politics—it did not survive as part of that public's textual memory. For example, Valerie Solanas's frequently excerpted and/or alluded to *SCUM Manifesto* went out of print in the early 1970s and has not seen steady publication since, although a small upsurge in public interest accompanied the release of 1996's *I Shot Andy Warhol*.[1] Shulamith Firestone's 1970 *The Dialectic of Sex*, rightly described by Morgan as "a basic building block" of contemporary feminism and a "classic articulation of the antithetical feminist position"[2] had been out of print for over 30 years before it was finally reissued in 2003. When radical feminist texts do survive, they survive in abbreviated form in anthologies such as Morgan's, or in anthologies such as Tanner's *Voices from Women's*

Liberation (1970) and Koedt, Levine, and Rapone's *Radical Feminism* (1973), which are themselves out of print. Recently, however, much progress has been made in the recovery and archiving of these texts, as evidenced by Miriam Schneir's *Feminism in Our Time* (1997), Barbara Crow's *Radical Feminism: A Documentary History* (2000), and the online archive of feminist texts at Duke University <http://scriptorium.lib.duke.edu/wlm/>.

In the midst of this larger progress in textual recovery, the absence of radical feminism looms as a significant silence in feminist compositionist scholarship, particularly since that scholarship has as one of its defining features the recovery of women's texts. Much recent work in rhetoric and composition assures us that scholars are both aware of the significance of silenced texts in rhetorical history and are also attempting to explore these silences in a variety of ways. In the midst of these conversations, however, feminist compositionists have remained silent themselves about the distinctly textual radical feminists and their rhetoric of political transformation. In this chapter, I hope to address this silence by providing an overview of the radical feminist movement in the late 1960s and early 1970s, particularly in the context of that movement's emphasis on textual agency. I explore the radical feminist movement in its curious multiplicity; one misapprehension of radical feminism is that it was somehow monolithic, when in fact as a movement it was quite fractious, with arguments coming from leftist, socialist, hard-line Marxist, and other ideological corners. Finally, I will provide a critical overview of the phenomenon of consciousness-raising groups within the radical feminist movement, particularly as those groups moved from self-revelation to collective (and often textual) action. Consciousness-raising was by no means an unproblematic activity for radical feminists, who regularly did battle over questions of content and purpose within discussion groups. It was generally accepted within radical feminist circles, however, that the expected outcome of a consciousness-raising group would be some sort of public action; often, these actions took the form of manifestos or underground publications, produced and written collaboratively and then distributed either on the street corner or through the mail, thanks to an underground publications network. Indeed, a radical feminist emphasis on written texts disseminated through an underground publication network served as a loose, superficially stable organization for the movement.

Many examinations of the emergence of second-wave feminism attempt to explain the phenomenon evolutionarily, emphasizing its connections with an originary student movement, civil rights movement, or first-wave feminist movement.[3] This originary explanation is a move born of necessity, demanded by a teleological approach to history that values the neat evolutionary trajectory from cause to effect. However, while it is certainly true that many late 1960s feminists cut their teeth in New Left activist groups such as Students for a Democratic Society (SDS) and the Student Nonviolent Coordinating Committee (SNCC), none of these evolutionary narratives explains satisfactorily just how second-wave feminism emerged when it did and in the ways it did. Specifically, none of these accounts can contain second-wave feminism's curious multiplicity of activist "movements," each with its own agenda for revolution or reform, and each with its own preferred method of achieving those ends. For example, the radical feminists' decision to make their own movement (outside of the organized left) created a rift between them and socialist feminists; similarly, the radical feminists distanced themselves from what they saw as the "assimilationist" mentality of liberal feminism—formal equality with men, according to radical feminists, "assumed that equality in an unjust society was worth fighting for."[4] However, from the hard-line Marxism and radical celibacy of Cell 16 to the pro-woman argument and abortion speakouts of Redstockings, radical feminists relied on the power of print technology and mass media, at least the underground variety, as a key means of enacting social change.

One example of both the textual imperative in radical feminism and the contentious nature of its beginnings is in Beverly Jones and Judith Brown's 1968 "Toward a Female Liberation Movement," a response to 1967's "An SDS Statement on the Liberation of Women," which was itself a key document in the history of second-wave feminism. In their article, which came to be known as "The Florida Paper," Jones and Brown criticize the women of the SDS for presenting their male counterparts with a "sweet-talking list of grievances" instead of taking their revolution into their own textual hands:

If the women in SDS want study committees on the problems of women, why don't they form them? If they want bibliographies, why

don't they gather them? If they want to protest University discrimination against women, why don't they do so? No one in SDS is going
to stop them. They can even use SDS auspices and publish in *New
Left Notes,* for a while anyway.[5]

Later, Jones and Brown write that it is an "urgent priority" that
women "support the newsletter and the journal and write out and
exchange our thoughts in these media."[6] The manifesto and its
cousins—the pamphlet and position statement—were invocations of
identity, a collective and decidedly temporary subjectivity formed for
the purpose of immediate and radical rhetorical action. Textuality in
public was very much a defining part of radical feminist existence, a
discursive existence based on creating temporary texts, engaging in
textual and physical "zap" actions, and gaining access to the means of
textual production.

In her 1977 *Going Too Far: The Personal Chronicle of a Feminist,*
Robin Morgan writes:

> Soon [after the publication of *Sisterhood is Powerful*] I faced a pile of
> requests from women for me to lecture, organize, advise, and agitate
> around the country. I recalled with a sense of irony how desperate
> we had been both in WITCH [Women's International Terrorist
> Conspiracy from Hell, a politico group] and at *Rat* to reach "those
> women out there"—and now the book actually had done it. How-
> ever much willful dullards might accuse literature of being hope-
> lessly elitist, even plain old-fashioned by [Marshall] McLuhan's
> standards, those first books from the new feminist wave certainly
> did have their effect.[7]

The ability of text to reach women "out there" certainly contributed to
the overall textual emphasis of radical feminism, and it is therefore
unfortunate that radical feminism has been buried or ignored in the
history of feminism and composition. These writerly, textual activists
offer much to those of us who believe in the power of collaborative and
collective intertextuality. Radical feminists wanted to unhinge the
overwhelming structure of repressive patriarchy, and one way they
planned to do it was through consciousness and text. In short, they
proposed a new literacy for women, a literacy heavily dependent on
temporary textual jumps into the political sphere.

DEFINITION, DISSENSUS, AND DISUNITY

"Radical feminism," writes Bonnie Kreps in 1968, "is called 'radical' because it is struggling to bring about really fundamental changes in our society. We, in this segment of the movement, do not believe that the oppression of women will be ended by giving them a bigger piece of the pie. . . . We believe that the pie itself is rotten."[8] Radical feminism formed from a split within the women's liberation movement between the "politicos," who maintained their ties with the organized left and its critique of capitalism, and the "feminists," who "argued against the subordination of women's liberation to the left, and blamed not only capitalism, but male supremacy and, later, men, for women's oppression."[9] Alternately, as Jo Freeman points out in *The Politics of Women's Liberation*, the split has been described as that between "women's rights" (reformist) and "women's liberation" (radical) branches. Freeman condemns this description of the split as a misconception about how the terms "radical" and "reformist" were deployed within the feminist movement. That is, she writes, some reformist groups "have a platform that would so completely change our society it would be unrecognizable. Other groups called 'radical' concentrate on the traditional female concerns of love, sex, children, and interpersonal relationships (although with nontraditional views)."[10] Freeman, a participant in the radical feminist movement herself (often writing under the pen name "Joreen"), distinguishes between the two branches of the movement . . . on the basis of "structure and style rather than ideology. . . . In general the older branch has used the traditional forms of political action while the younger branch has been experimental."[11]

Regardless of how the initial split is described, however, by the end of the 1960s, "feminism" had come to replace "women's liberation" as the general descriptor of the movement, the "politicos" had become "socialist feminists" or "liberal feminists" depending on their allegiances, and the "feminists" had become the "radical feminists," who insisted that the first, foundational oppression in human history was sexism. At their founding meeting in December 1969, for example, the New York Radical Feminists (NYRF) adopted a manifesto stating:

> the oppression of women [is] a fundamental political oppression wherein women are categorized as an inferior class based upon their sex. . . . [The] purpose of male chauvinism is primarily to obtain

psychological ego satisfaction, and only secondarily does this manifest itself in economic relationships. For this reason we do not
believe that capitalism, or any other economic system, is the cause
of female oppression, nor do we believe that female oppression will
disappear as a result of a purely economic revolution.[12]

Similarly, the "Redstockings Manifesto," written by another radical
feminist group the same year, argues that male supremacy is the "oldest, most basic form of domination."[13] The idea of an autonomous
women's movement dedicated solely to eradicating sexism was by no
means accepted throughout the feminist community, however. As
Morgan points out, "even if a large room is crammed strictly with radical feminists . . . there is still sufficient disagreement *within* the fold to
boggle the mind," and cites such issues as marriage, lesbianism, ageism,
racism, and group structure.[14] Indeed, these disagreements led to the
very formation of groups like the NYRF, WITCH, and Redstockings,
each of which had emerged from the political factionalism that dissolved a larger umbrella group, New York Radical Women (NYRW),
founded in 1967 by Pam Allen and Shulamith Firestone.

In spite of their other political differences, these groups and others
shared a belief that personal experience—and in particular, *women's* personal experience—served as the only "authority" upon which to base political action. An important corollary to that belief was the argument that
women were fundamentally the same, or that they at least had enough in
common to unite them in a mass movement, if only they were made aware
of those commonalities. In "About My Consciousness Raising," for example, Redstockings member Barbara Susan relies on what Rita Mae Brown
calls "mystique of unity" that informed much radical feminist theorizing.
Susan writes that in order to form a powerful movement, feminism must
answer the needs "of all women."[15] While Redstockings recognize differences in class and race, Susan claims, they also hope:

> that consciousness raising in groups of women who are not the same
> will help us to understand each other and help us all in building a
> movement which answers to the needs of more than just the most
> privileged woman. Our analysis is an expanding one, it changes as
> more and more women enter the movement and contribute their
> knowledge and experience thereby widening and correcting our
> understanding of oppression.[16]

Once women were united, political differences within radical feminist groups determined how that unity might be put to use. While Redstockings, as radical feminists, were committed to an autonomous women's movement focusing exclusively on sexism, other groups saw women's unity as a means to connect with a larger political movement. In a 1969 issue of *No More Fun and Games*, Cell 16's newsletter, Mary Ann Weathers writes that Black women have been using all of their energy to "liberate" Black men; however, she argues, "if you yourself are not free, how can you 'liberate' someone else?"[17] Once women are free, according to Weathers, feminists can direct their energy to the liberation movement at large, since women's liberation is "a strategy for an eventual tie-up with the entire revolutionary movement consisting of women, men, and children."[18] Weathers also argues for forming links of commonality to women across culture, race, and ethnicity:

> All women suffer oppression, even white women, particularly poor white women, and especially Indian, Mexican, Puerto Rican, Oriental and Black American women whose oppression is tripled by any of the above mentioned. But we do have female's oppression in common. This means that we can begin to talk to other women with this common factor and start building links with them and thereby build and transform the revolutionary force we are now beginning to amass.[19]

Like Cell 16, the Redstockings believed in a unity of women across difference, writing in their manifesto that they "identify with all women" and that they "repudiate all economic, racial, educational, or status privileges that divide [them] from other women."[20] We should not dismiss these calls for unity uncritically, for they are based less on an essentialist conception of women's identity than a constructivist conception of the self within patriarchy.

It is important to note that radical feminists themselves problematized the idea of "unity" among women from the start. The first critiques of women's unity came from within the movement, most notably from the Furies, a group that challenged radical feminism's classism, and the Radicalesbians, a group that challenged radical feminism's homophobia.[21] Further, such calls for unity depended less on essentialism than on constructivism; that is, radical feminists based much of their theory on Simone de Beauvoir's assertion that "one is not born, but rather becomes, a woman." Firestone was so influenced by de Beauvoir's work that she dedicated her own *The Dialectic of Sex: The Case for Feminist Revolution* to her. Juliet Mitchell, writing in 1966 on the eve of the radical feminist movement, calls de Beauvoir's *The Second Sex* "the greatest single contribution" on the subject of women's oppression because it "fuses the 'economic' and 'reproductive' explanations of women's subordination by a psychological interpretation of both."[22] The notion of becoming, constructing, or performing gender was thus well in place by the end of the 1960s.

The constructivist leanings of the radical women's movement are evident in the appearance of what is known as the "pro-woman" argument, typified in Kreps's 1968 "Radical Feminism 1," a brief to the Royal Commission on the Status of Women in Canada that was published subsequently as part of *Notes from the Second Year*. *Notes* was an annual compilation of radical women's writings, published for three years by New York Radical Women. *Notes from the First Year* (1968) and *Notes from the Second Year* (1969) were edited by Firestone and Anne Koedt; *Notes from the Third Year* (1970), the final volume, was edited by Koedt, Ellen Levine, and Anita Rapone, who published selections from the *Notes* series in their 1973 anthology *Radical Feminism*. Like many radical feminists, Kreps draws from de Beauvoir's assertion; specifically, Kreps writes that to "understand woman's so-called 'nature,' we must . . . examine her situation: her history, the myths about her, her social environment, her education, and so forth."[23] Further, Kreps argues that the "economic discrimination against the working woman is highly conducive to her seeing marriage as a liberation from ill-paid drudgery."[24] The pro-woman argument, advanced most notably by the Redstockings, insisted that women were not "brainwashed" into marriage and childrearing (as had been argued by the politicos), but instead chose it as a strategy for coping with systemic oppression. In their 1969 manifesto, the Redstockings write that they "reject the idea that women consent to or are to blame for their own oppression. Women's submission is not the result of brainwashing, stupidity, or mental illness but of continual, daily pressure from men."[25]

There were important challenges to this view of unified (though constructed) womanhood, challenges that were based then (as many are now) on issues of race, class, and sexual orientation. In "For Sadie and Maude," her contribution to *Sisterhood is Powerful*, Eleanor Holmes Norton writes that:

our goals and theirs [white feminists'] in their general outlines are the same, but black women confront a task that is as delicate as it is revolutionary. For black women are part of a preeminent struggle whose time has come—the fight for black liberation. If women were suddenly to achieve equality with men tomorrow, black women would continue to carry the entire array of utterly oppressive handicaps associated with race.[26]

Likewise, in "Revolution Begins at Home," Furies collective members Coletta Reid and Charlotte Bunch address the particular ways in which middle-class assumptions of superiority oppress working-class women in the movement, arguing that "[bringing] down the male supremacist system in this country will not be a possibility until we stop acting out our class supremacist attitudes on the women with whom we're building a movement."[27] The authors write that "looking down with scorn or pity at those whose emotions are not repressed or who can't rap out abstract theories in thirty seconds flat reeks of our class arrogance and self-righteousness."[28] Brown, another Fury, writes that to a working-class woman,

> this constant preoccupation with one's feelings and the difficulty of changing is a luxury she could never afford. . . . She had to do many unpleasant things that middle class women complain about endlessly, like exploitative jobs, just to survive. Endlessly analyzing and discussing your feelings is another way to keep control, which involves both out-talking people and using your feelings as excuses.[29]

Even some of the cherished causes of second-wave feminism were not enough to make activists rally 'round the unified feminist flag. As Echols points out in *Daring to Be Bad*, even the Equal Rights Amendment was not supported by all factions within the feminist movement—indeed, some feminists viewed it with outright suspicion. Brown writes, for example, that the ERA will "defuse the revolutionary wing of the Women's Liberation Movement and . . . open vistas of establishment opportunity for professional women"; once the ERA is passed, Brown argues, middle-class women will again "neglect the 'dangerous' issues the revolutionaries have raised," because they "do not begin to question the basic structure of our nation, they are gaining too many benefits from Wall Street and its colonies."[30] What is important in this instance is not the ERA, but the idea that dissensus and disunity has always played a part in the women's liberation movement; we are not the first to critique the radical feminists for their valorization of "universal woman."[31] While it is true that radical feminists tended to subordinate race, class, and sexual orientation to gender, it is important to note, with Echols, that such "hyperbolic" subordination was itself a response to the New Left's subordination of gender to issues of race and class.[32] It is equally important to note that even though the radical feminists themselves came late to the critique, the critique was already in place.

As noted by many critics, the roots of second-wave feminism are buried deep in an uncritical universalist discourse that is the discourse of racism, classism, and homophobia. These discourses of exclusion informed many of the texts and actions that followed, including texts and actions that ultimately dissolved the radical movement into something more liberal but not necessarily more aware. Radical feminism certainly does not escape these discourses, any more than *liberal* feminism could when Betty Friedan, in 1970, raised the specter of a "lavender menace" in order to purge lesbians from the women's movement.[33] To be sure, then, we must view radical feminism critically, paying particular attention to the overzealous claims of universality made, ironically, at the expense of women's lived experience—the very experience that formed the underpinning of radical feminist beliefs in consciousness-raising and the pro-woman argument. The critiques of radical feminism point to blind spots in the "pure theory" of the radical feminists, blind spots that often accompany liberatory movements (e.g., the tendency to colonize the colonized in order to "liberate" them). It is important, therefore, to have textual and pedagogical discourses that encourage their own critique. Paulo Freire's work provides a case in point; his work is often criticized, and rightly so, for its sexism. Freire, according to hooks, like other progressive thinkers and political leaders, "constructs a phallocentric paradigm of liberation—wherein freedom and the experience of patriarchal manhood are always linked as though they are one and the same."[34] However, hooks also argues that "Freire's own model of critical pedagogy invites a critical interrogation of this flaw in the work. But critical interrogation is not the same as dismissal."[35] The radical feminist actions of consciousness-raising and textual production also invite their own critical interrogation; it is my argument that we have dismissed them much too soon, if we have considered them at all.

CONSCIOUSNESS-RAISING AND THE
PROBLEM OF (ANTI)STRUCTURE

One story that we tell about second-wave feminism is that it was a movement rife with consciousness-raising "rap" groups, groups composed of mostly white, mostly middle-class women in need of cheap therapy with a woman-centered spin. For example, in "Valuing the Personal: Feminist Concerns for the Writing Classroom," Carol Mattingly explores the difficulty of reconciling feminists' support for personal experience writing with the less heterogeneous context of the composition classroom. Mattingly writes that "some difficulties have evolved because teachers have often transposed practices that had proven successful in earlier, more homogeneous settings onto the more diverse writing classroom."[36] Mattingly, like other feminist compositionists, draws a direct link between "feminist theory's interest in personal experience" and "women's consciousness-raising groups of the late 1960s and early 1970s."[37] However, it is important to remember that consciousness-raising groups were more than trouble-free gatherings of like-minded individuals, each sharing her personal experience uncritically. As Susan writes, such groups formed for the purpose not only of sharing personal experience, but of theorizing that experience in an effort to change social conditions:

> Consciousness raising is a way of forming a political analysis on information we can trust is true. That information is our experience. It is difficult to understand how our oppression is political (organized) unless we first remove it from the area of personal problems. Unless we talk to each other about our so called personal problems and see how many of our problems are shared by other people, we won't be able to see how these problems are rooted in politics.[38]

Consciousness-raising was viewed with suspicion by politicos and radicals alike, and so its status today as that-which-typifies-second-wave-feminism is somewhat ironic. Freeman, for example, notes that members of the National Organization for Women (NOW) avoided consciousness-raising initially, in part because it was a "phenomenon closely associated with the younger branch of the movement."[39] However, NOW veterans did see some benefits in setting up consciousness-raising

groups, since such groups could serve as the venue for the feminist education needed before feminist activity, and thus older members would
not have to spend so much time going over old ground with new members.[40] This suspicion of consciousness-raising groups was not limited to
NOW members; indeed, Morgan writes that WITCH, a group of
politico women devoted to "zap" actions like hexing the New York Stock
Exchange and bridal fairs, also disdained consciousness-raising groups.
The Women's International Conspiracy from Hell (WITCH) devoted
itself to guerrilla theater protests, even at the expense of other feminists;
it was widely rumored that WITCH members defaced other feminist
groups' banners and planned to drag Firestone from the stage during her
speech at the 1968 Counter-Inaugural Protest.[41] WITCH members
"identified politically with the confrontational tactics of the male Left
and stylistically with the clownish proto-anarchism of such groups as the
Yippies. . . . It seemed intolerable that we should sit around 'just talking'
when there was so much to be done."[42] Mattingly's concern with "right
method" in using personal experience, then, was also a concern of both
organizers and critics of rap groups, all of whom worried that less political women might use the groups to (misguidedly) find *individual* solutions to *systemic* problems.

The "Redstockings Manifesto" devotes some time to arguing
against introspection as its own end, claiming that consciousness-raising "is not 'therapy,' which implies the existence of individual solutions
and falsely assumes that the male-female relationship is purely personal, but the only method by which we can ensure that our program
for liberation is based on the concrete realities of our lives."[43] Similarly,
a circa-1970 pamphlet entitled "Consciousness Raising" claims that
the purpose of consciousness-raising is to "clean out your head,"
"uncork and redirect your anger," "learn to understand other women,"
and to "discover that your personal problem is not only yours."[44] Susan's
experience is instructive; she notes that a Redstockings consciousness-
raising session on abortion led her to demand that her husband take
more responsibility for birth control.[45] Susan's situation was part of a
larger collective action, however; in her consciousness-raising group,
the members "came to realize that it was not only the abortion laws
that had to be repealed, but that something was wrong with the whole
idea of men calling themselves experts on problems that they would
never have to face. In fact we found that we were opposed to the whole
idea of experts."[46] Soon after this session, the Redstockings took col-

lective action and interrupted the February 1969 New York legislative hearings on abortion reform, in which the state used fourteen men and a nun as its expert witnesses. Redstockings Kathie Sarachild and Ellen Willis disrupted the meeting to the point that the legislators had to adjourn and meet in executive session.[47] A month later, the Redstockings began holding their own hearings, which involved women testifying about their own illegal abortions.[48]

While consciousness-raising was a key contribution—indeed, some would argue *the* key contribution—made by radical feminists, its history and deployment is not nearly as untroubledly homogeneous as this story would have us believe. Echols writes that from its beginnings in NYRW, feminist consciousness-raising stirred controversy; while NYRW founder Pam Allen wanted rap groups to be more structured, sessions were often "spirited and unstructured" and group members "freely interrupted one another."[49] Further, Echols writes, the unstructured, confrontational method of group work allowed some women—Sarachild and Firestone among others—to dominate discussions, thus creating the conditions for two of the most divisive issues within radical feminism: the related problems of structure and leadership.[50] The Redstockings wrote that one of their founding principles was the commitment to "internal democracy," which meant providing every woman an "equal chance to participate, assume responsibility, and develop her political potential."[51] In reality, internal democracy often meant chaos and an inability to act as a group. In her 1979 *A Group Called Women: Sisterhood & Symbolism in the Feminist Movement*, a case study of second-wave feminism, Joan Cassell writes that:

> the operating principles of a women's liberation group included radical egalitarianism; self-actualization; group decision making; and a ban on leadership, structure, and the individual exercise of power. . . . Power was rarely discussed; instead, members talked of 'the way women did things'—with an assumption that the way women did things was cooperatively—as opposed to the way men did things, which was coercively. . . . Ability and expertise were on occasion condemned as hierarchical, and feminist professionalization discussed as "ripping off the movement."[52]

Cassell describes a phenomenon to which she refers as "decision by exhaustion," by which group members eventually move to take action.

Decision-by-exhaustion, according to Cassell, "was in line with the high value placed on consensus in the group and the conscious avoidance of formal structure, including the avoidance of special roles and mechanisms to facilitate decision making."[53] By the time the group had actually agreed on a course of action, Cassell writes, "so many proposals had been discussed so many times that it was difficult to remember exactly who had decided what. . . . Decision by exhaustion, then, was (or was perceived to be) decision by consensus."[54] Freeman notes a similar tension within consciousness-raising groups that attempt to move toward specific political action. In her 1972 "The Tyranny of Structurelessness," Freeman (writing under her pseudonym "Joreen") argues that the "leaderless, structureless groups" only work as long as the main goal and method of the feminist movement is consciousness-raising; however, once activists want to move from consciousness-raising to more concrete action, structureless organization becomes a hindrance; individual groups "usually floundered because most groups were unwilling to change their structure when they changed their tasks."[55]

While there is marked disagreement about whether the loose structure of consciousness-raising groups could lend itself to concrete action, it does seem clear that feminists of various stripes intended to structure consciousness-raising groups as part of a more effective political organization. Cassell writes, for example, that the NYRF attempted to institute a three-stage process to transform a loose network of small consciousness-raising groups into a mass movement working for social change. The three stages are (1) a small group moving from consciousness-raising to reading movement literature; (2) the group then applying to join the NYRF as a "cell" group; and (3) the group, upon acceptance into the NYRF, having "full autonomy to undertake political actions."[56] The plan did not work, writes Cassell, and it is at least partially for that reason that the radical feminists, unlike NOW members, have no formal structure that can help link women to the women's movement as a whole.[57] An outline for a workshop prepared by Sarachild encourages a similar three-stage structural approach to consciousness-raising, during which a group moves from a "bitch session" cell group to direct political action and then to networking with other groups. The "bitch session" serves as a place not only for women to speak about their individual experiences, but also to tie those experiences to a radical feminist analysis of patriarchal oppression; at the end of this stage of a consciousness-raising group, each woman is trained to organize other cell groups.[58] According to Sarachild, the second stage of a consciousness-raising group consists of consciousness-raising actions such as "zaps" (movie benefits, attacks on cultural events, stickers, buttons, etc.), "consciousness programs" such as newspapers, storefronts, and communes, and communications with mainstream mass media.[59] In the last stage, according to Sarachild, consciousness-raising groups help members start new groups and also participate in "intra-group communication and actions" such as monthly meetings and conferences.[60]

The circa-1970 "Consciousness Raising" pamphlet mentioned previously, like the documents produced by the NYRF and Sarachild, provided a topic list and course of study for consciousness-raising groups. The topics range from relationships to socialization, from aging to sexuality; they move from a focus on one's individual interactions with men ("Discuss your relationships with men as they have evolved. Have you noticed any recurring patterns?") to a broader social understanding of one's gender constructedness ("Problems of growing up as a girl—socialization: Were you treated differently from your brother?"). Importantly, the suggested course of study ends with a week-12 discussion of what each woman wants the feminist movement to accomplish.[61] Part of the radical feminist idea of consciousness-raising, as evidenced in the writings of the radical feminists themselves, was not only to teach women to think critically about their own experience, but also to interrogate the feminist movement (and the rap group as part of that movement). As Baxandall writes of a Redstockings consciousness-raising group:

> Some spoke animatedly for ten minutes, others whispered a few sentences. We would challenge one another, often too roughly, but this harshness actually helped us learn from each other. We interrupted each other when someone said something that didn't sound authentic, or was antiwoman, racist, or elitist. In this process, we learned from each other.[62]

RADICAL FEMINIST MANIFESTOS AND MEDIA

The emphasis on text as the expected outcome of group formation and consciousness-raising was the purview of radical feminists, a phenomenon noted by Maren Lockwood Carden when she explains the methodology behind *The New Feminist Movement,* her case study of the feminist movement. Writing in 1974—soon after she had completed her own participant observation of the movement—Carden cautions that most of the women "who put out movement magazines and newspapers and, less commonly, newsletters, belong to one of the radical wings of the new feminism and are by no means representative of either Women's Liberation or Women's Rights."[63] Indeed, it seems fitting that the radical feminists, with their emphasis on group work, were responsible for the wealth of movement literature. Consciousness-raising groups, structured or not, provided a context in which women could work collectively and critically to change their condition; an important part of that work was related directly to writing. Not surprisingly, then, much radical feminist work was written collaboratively. If that work was published by any member groups of the burgeoning feminist publications network— and given the less-than-stellar reporting of the women's movement in the mass media, chances are it was—then it was published collaboratively, too. As Judith Hole and Ellen Levine note, many feminist publications were run collectively, from editorial decisions to layout to typesetting to bookkeeping.[64] The collaborative group that wrote the texts was often the same group that published the texts, the most trenchant example being the *Notes* series published (and written) by different incarnations of NYRW.

A key part of radical feminist textuality is its policy of "male exclusion" as a matter of principle when dealing with mainstream media. Freeman reports that all journalists, regardless of sex, had some difficulty covering early second-wave feminist activities.[65] The mainstream media had shown itself quite capable of distorting movement activities; a case in point is the ongoing "bra-burning feminist" red herring. The source of the story is the protest of the Miss America Pageant in 1968, during which feminists tossed a number of symbols of traditional womanhood—high-heeled shoes, bras, girdles, curlers, and copies of *Playboy* and *Cosmopolitan,* among other things, into a trash can and planned to set it on fire. Atlantic City, however, prevented the burning for fear of destroying the city's flammable boardwalks.[66]

Because of the misreporting of various protest activities such as the previously mentioned one, most younger feminists were distrustful of the mainstream media and would not talk to reporters at all. The politico factions of the women's liberation movement held fast to that principle; radical feminists, on the other hand, concentrated on creating an autonomous women's media (at the same time that they made use of the underground left media) and would also use the mainstream media with caution. In their statement of organizing principles, first published in *Notes from the Second Year*, the NYRF write:

> We will work only with women reporters but will inform and penal-ize in an appropriate manner any reporter and medium that, for whatever reason, in tone or substance, presents distorted or partial information about our group. We will also seek to form a strong coalition with other women's rights groups in order to deal more effectively with the problems and potential of the media.[67]

The radical feminists were as good as their word. If they did consent to interviews, they frequently demanded both anonymity and editorial control of the final copy (the latter demand was always denied); and if they were observed without their consent, women's liberationists would eject reporters from meetings and destroy their notes, microphones, and film. Eventually, however, more media-savvy activists would give female reporters "reams of material to read, arrange interviews and group discussions for their benefit, and direct them to good sources of information."[68] According to Freeman, the policy of male exclusion worked subversively, constituting a shock tactic that changed how mainstream media treated its female employees. She writes that as more female reporters were assigned to cover movement activities, "they often found themselves much more involved in the ideas of the movement than they intended. . . . Virtually all the initial stories in *Time, Life, Newsweek*, etc., are personal conversion stories."[69] Freeman further notes that as the publication of these conversion stories contin-ued, women "writers, researchers, and even secretaries became con-scious of their secondary role on their publications and began protest-ing for better conditions and forming their own small groups."[70]

Not only did feminists indirectly affect mainstream media, they more directly changed the alternative press, primarily through actions like the 1970 takeover of the leftist publication *Rat*. Because of the entrenched sexism of *Rat*'s (all-male) editorial staff, Morgan had refused to continue writing for the paper. After the women of *Rat* took over the paper, they requested help from the women's liberation movement. Morgan writes that the help, coming from all parts of New York's feminist community, "knew precisely nothing about type-setting, layout, advertising, dealing with printers, or distribution. But we put out a paper. And the first 'Women's *Rat*' became a reality."[71] Morgan notes that there were already feminist newspapers in exis-tence, most notably *Everywoman*, *It Ain't Me Babe*, and *Off Our Backs*. However, she writes, the *Rat* action:

> was the first time women had seized a male-run newspaper, and the action created ripples all over the Left, with women following suit in other cities and taking over their local underground media. . . . It was not until after that first issue had been put together by women that we ourselves realized we weren't about to give the paper back. We intended to keep it, in fact, as a radical newspaper written and pub-lished collectively by women.[72]

Hole and Levine write that even though there was some controversy about whether the new *Rat* was a feminist paper or an underground paper run by women, the takeover itself "was looked upon as a 'break-through' in the political relationship between radical women and radi-cal men."[73] Specifically, they cite key changes in the male-run under-ground media made because of the increasing power of the women's liberation movement; writing in 1971, they note that many of the papers no longer accepted pornographic advertising, that they regularly ran women's liberation columns, and that most of them "have turned at least one entire issue over to women, in content and editorship."[74] Most importantly, however, feminists not only changed mainstream and underground male-run media, but they created their own independent publication network.

In *The New Feminist Movement*, Carden traces the growth of radi-cal feminist print culture, noting that between 1968 and 1971, the num-ber of feminist newsletters, magazines, and newspapers increased from two to sixty,[75] while Hole and Levine insist that by the beginning of 1971 "there were over one hundred women's liberation journals and newspa-pers being published."[76] Carden, Hole, and Levine do agree that the first two feminist periodicals of note were Chicago's *Voice of the Women's Lib-eration Movement (VWLM)*, with its national subscriber base, and *No More Fun and Games*, which was written and distributed locally by Boston's Cell 16. The national newsletter, *VWLM*, was founded in

March 1968 as a three-page mimeograph edited by Freeman; it grew quickly in size and circulation, made use of a different editor each issue, and "was one of the most useful organizational tools of the movement" until June 1969.[77] Freeman writes that the "revolving editors":

> gave most issues away free to anyone indicating any interest whatso-
> ever in the women's movement and placed many on bookstore
> shelves. . . . Its purpose was to reach any potential sympathizer in
> order to let her know that there were others who thought as she did
> and that she was not isolated or crazy. It also functioned to put
> women in contact with other like-minded women in the same area
> and thus stimulated the formation of new groups. . . . The *Vwlm* grew
> from 200 copies the first issue to 2,000 the seventh and last; from 6
> pages to 25. It was finally killed because the work of keeping it up
> had grown too big to handle.[78]

While women behind the NYRW's *Notes from the First Year* did not give their publication away, they did enforce a pricing policy that charged men "for the privilege of reading the magazine."[79] The *Notes* series, which began in 1968 under the editorship of Firestone and Koedt, sold for $0.50 to women and $1.00 to men, a pricing decision that served as "political education"; while the NYRW realized that men could just get women to buy *Notes* for them, they wanted to illustrate "the true nature of the female role by reverse example as well as the high price of independence."[80] Thus, the texts were made and sold cheaply, but still served a political purpose. This surplus of text can be explained through the radical emphasis on "spreading the word" through manifesto-writing and reading, and also through the activists' general distrust of mass media. One of the first steps a new feminist group took was to write its own position statement or manifesto; in fact, manifesto- and group-formation often seem to have been concurrent actions. For example, "Politics of the Ego: A Manifesto for N.Y. Radical Feminists," was adopted by the NYRF at its founding meeting in 1969, just as Kate Millett's "Sexual Politics: A Manifesto for Revolution" was "written in 1968 in connection with the organizational meeting of the first women's liberation group at Columbia University."[81] Soon after manifestos were written, they were distributed as leaflets or pamphlets through on-street sales or were included as part of new feminist journals like the NYRW's *Notes* series.

It is clear, then, that a radical feminist emphasis on anti-structure and its suspicion of "leaders" might lead rather naturally to both uncredited and collaborative authorship of manifestos and other texts. For example, Morgan writes that when the *Rat* collective "decided it was elitist for any member to sign her name to her work," she dutifully left her byline off of her articles.[82] Further, she writes, the collective expected her to eschew individual style in favor of collective voice. She writes:

> When the collective, a few months later, criticized me for writing in a style which was apparently still identifiable to our readers. . . . I even tried to worsen my writing: I spelled America with *three* k's instead of one, as I had done previously in the Left; I dropped my g's in print; I peppered my articles with words like imperialism, running-dog-of-a-capitalist-swine, and other phrases which would have given George Eliot the vapours. But this still was not sufficient, and at one meeting it was suggested that I not write for the paper at all—but not quit, either (that would be a cop-out); I should stay and work on proof-reading, layout, and distribution—just not write.[83]

Similarly, the Black Women's Liberation Group signs its "Statement on Birth Control" (an argument that using the birth control pill is not, as some Black men had claimed, a type of genocide) as "two welfare recipients, two housewives, a domestic, a grandmother, a psychotherapist, and others who read, agreed, but did not help to compose."[84] The NYRF's "Politics of the Ego," on the other hand, is signed "A.K.," and thus one might assume that the author is Koedt (one of the group's founders)—the point is, however, that individual authorship was held in suspicion and had to be mitigated through the use of initials and pseudonyms if it happened at all.

The collaboratively authored "Redstockings Manifesto" (1969) is perhaps the most frequently anthologized (and thus most well-known) of the radical feminist manifestos. Founded by Firestone and Ellen Willis in early 1969, the Redstockings were staunch advocates of consciousness-raising and public actions such as abortion speakouts. The manifesto itself is divided into seven sections, each one a brief, to-the-point articulation of key aspects of Redstockings' philosophy, namely the ideas of male supremacy as the foundational oppression and the pro-woman argument. The argumentative strategy contained in the "Redstockings Manifesto" would come to typify many such documents;

the strategy is an inductive one, defining the group first, then women (as an oppressed class), and then men (as oppressors). They write that it is an "illusion" that a man and a woman can work out their relationship individually, as two unique personalities; in fact, they write, "every such relationship is a *class* relationship, and the conflicts between individual men and women are *political* conflicts that can only be solved collectively."[85] After rejecting the possibility of blaming either institutions or women themselves for oppression, the Redstockings claim to "identify with all women" for the purpose of promoting an activist-oriented unity. Consciousness-raising forms a key part of this process of identification. The Redstockings write that since all existing ideologies are products of "male supremacist culture," women must "question every generalization and accept none that are not confirmed by our experience."[86] To that end, the Redstockings see their chief task as developing "female class consciousness through sharing experience and publicly exposing the sexist foundation of all our institutions."[87] This absolute emphasis on consciousness-raising and the pro-woman argument ultimately created divisions within the group; its manifesto, however, remains one of the clearer articulations of a radical feminist stance.

By the end of 1969, Redstockings had itself split into several factions, including the NYRF. NYRF's manifesto, like that of the Redstockings, typifies the genre; it begins by defining "radical feminism" by its purpose (which is to organize women to destroy the "sex class system"[88]), identifies male oppression as the primary division of humanity, and, after a brief explication of how male oppression operates within our culture, it advocates a specific action. "The Politics of the Ego" repeats the radical feminist admonition against finding individual solutions for systemic problems, especially in the case of male-female relationships. According to the NYRF, the political oppression of women "has its own class dynamic; and that dynamic must be understood in terms previously called 'non-political'—namely the politics of the ego."[89] According to the NYRF, it is the destruction of women's egos—accomplished through an inauthentic and exploitative "love" relationship—that enables men to rob women of their ability to resist.[90] The specific action demanded by the NYRF is that women "fully develop a new dialectic of sex class—an analysis of the way in which sexual identity and institutions reinforce one another."[91] This challenge would be taken up soon by one of the group's founders, ex-NYRW member and ex-Redstocking Shulamith Firestone, whose *The Dialectic of Sex*

appeared in print in 1970. Firestone's work recasts dialectic material-
ism to emphasize "sex class" rather than "economic class"; advances in
reproductive technology, she writes, have made it possible to finally liberate humanity. She writes:

> So that just as to assure elimination of economic classes requires the
> revolt of the underclass (the proletariat) and, in a temporary dictator-
> ship, their seizure of the means of *production*, so to assure the elimina-
> tion of sexual classes requires the revolt of the underclass (women) and
> the seizure of control of *reproduction:* not only the full restoration of
> women to ownership of their own bodies, but also their (temporary)
> seizure of control of human fertility—the new population biology as
> well as all the social institutions of childbearing and childrearing.[92]

Millett's individually authored "Sexual Politics: A Manifesto for
Revolution" (a precursor to her 1970 book)[93] also refigures the politics
of male-female relationships, particularly the relationships within a
nuclear family. Millett argues that "[when] one group rules another, the
relationship between the two is political. When such an arrangement
is carried out over a long period of time it develops an ideology (feu-
dalism, racism, etc.). All historical civilizations are patriarchies: their
ideology is male supremacy."[94] Further, according to Millett, a "Sexual
Revolution" would bring about eight conditions: the end of sexual
repression; unisex temperament and behavior; reexamination of "masculine" and "feminine" traits; the end of "sex role and sex status"; the
end of the oppression of the young "under the patriarchal proprietary
family"; "bisex," or the end of normative heterosexuality; the end of
"hatred" sexuality (violence, warfare, etc.); "the attainment of the
female sex to freedom and full human status."[95] Like the NYRF manifesto, "Sexual Politics" first identifies the context for political action
(enumerating instances of systemic male oppression) and then calls for
political action—in this case, a sexual revolution.

Other groups called for revolution, but had a more violent one in
mind. The "Southern Female Rights Union Program for Female Liberation," written in 1970 after Cell 16 founder Roxanne Dunbar
moved from Boston to New Orleans, is a collaborative work that presents its demands first and its context last. While Dunbar (the
acknowledged leader of the group) can be viewed as more of a politico
than a radical feminist—and in fact Echols argues that Dunbar and

Cell 16 were the "prototypical" *cultural* feminists—the "Program" insists, with the radicals, that sexism is "the oldest form of institution-alized oppression."[96] In this piece, the Southern Female Rights Union (SFRU) demands free, noncompulsory childcare; adequate guaranteed annual income; an end to sexual (and racial) discrimination in employ-ment; free self-defense training for women; withdrawal of "deadly" hormonal birth control pills from the market; and a new media code of ethics, which would be committed to ending sexist representations. The SFRU suggests taxing the rich to pay for these programs; should those in power balk at funding the programs, "women must fight and act upon our demands" and thus *take* human rights.[97]

It is perhaps not surprising that groups like Cell 16 and the SFRU advocated a proactive stance toward male oppression (Cell 16 had as part of its agenda karate lessons for women), influenced as they were by Solanas's 1967 *SCUM* (Society for Cutting Up Men) *Manifesto.* Indeed, Echols describes Dunbar's thinking as a "strange mélange of Marx, Mao, de Beauvoir, and Solanas."[98] SCUM was a fictional group, described by Solanas herself as "a state of mind."[99] The manifesto itself, as former Cell 16 member Dana Densmore recalls, was a "wild, crazy, man-hating diatribe filled with energy, nastiness, and taboo truths."[100] Cell 16 and The Feminists, a group led by Ti-Grace Atkinson, valued Solanas's critique of sex and sexual desire as something from which women needed to be liberated; however, the *SCUM Manifesto* was not overwhelmingly accepted into radical circles, and had little impact until it was excerpted in Morgan's *Sisterhood is Powerful.* Firestone, for example, recalls that she did not particularly value Solanas's book because "it had a dangerous leaning towards what would become matriarchalist theory in the women's movement, a glorification of women as they are in their oppressed state."[101] Solanas herself had no ties to the women's liberation groups in New York, and Echols notes that most members of NYRW "knew next to nothing about Solanas until she shot and nearly killed Pop artist Andy Warhol in June 1968."[102] After her arrest and subsequent trial, however, Solanas became an icon of sorts, since radical feminists saw her confinement in a mental hospital as indicative of the larger crime of male oppression. Densmore writes that she and Dunbar believed that the "ideology of patriarchy" made it so that "when a man shoots someone, he is either justified or a criminal, but when a woman shoots someone, well, she must be crazy, since women don't do such things."[103]

This conception of Solanas as insane contributes, I think, to the continued fascination with the *SCUM Manifesto* as a curiosity of the "man-hating feminists," a stereotype too often invoked in knee-jerk characterizations of the women's liberation movement, even though the manifesto itself was not produced as part of the women's movement. Solanas's self-published manifesto, however, like other manifestos, has clear demands within a clear context of male oppression, which is evident from the first paragraph:

> Life in this society being, at best, an utter bore and no aspect of society being at all relevant to women, there remains to civic-minded, responsible, thrill-seeking females only to overthrow the government, eliminate the money system, institute complete automation, and destroy the male sex.[104]

Like other, more organized radical feminists, Solanas believed that the only successful women's movement was one that had revolution (rather than reform) in mind. She writes that "SCUM will not picket, demonstrate, march, or strike to attempt to achieve its ends. Such tactics are for nice, genteel ladies who scrupulously take only such action as is guaranteed to be ineffective. . . . SCUM is out to destroy the system, not attain certain rights within it."[105] Solanas's method of distributing her text—selling mimeographed copies of it on the streets of Greenwich Village—was also typical of the radical women's movement approach to text, an approach which emphasized a group's self-publication and distribution of text through informal networking.

The manifesto, with its clear purpose and context, its ambiguous authorship, and its very public audience, eventually became a preferred method of communicating radical feminism to women "out there." This emphasis on public, purposeful textuality was a hallmark of the women's liberation movement, evidenced by its textual beginnings in letters to the editor of the SDS newsletter; "An SDS Statement on the Liberation of Women," written in response to outrageous sexism at the SDS's 1967 National Convention; "To the Women of the Left," a 1967 manifesto written by Chicago women in response to outrageous sexism at the National Conference for New Politics, at about the same time that Solanas was distributing the *SCUM Manifesto;* the 1968 publication of *VWLM;* and the increasing number of manifestos, each one serving not only as a statement of a group's purpose, but also as a statement of that group's *identity* as radical feminist. The establishment of a national textual network, and the increased emphasis on rhetoric as a means of group identification, did much to create a larger and at least superficially more coherent movement. As Freeman notes, while the radical feminists did not have prominent organizations such as NOW, they did have "an often tenuous network of personal contacts and feminist publications" that linked "thousands of sister chapters around the country" through "numerous publications, personal correspondence, and cross-country travelers."[106] Similarly, Hole and Levine write that the main reason that the women's liberation movement expanded so quickly in its early days was that "it had ready access to an existing underground communications network" with which many women's liberationists were familiar, given their background in other liberation movements.[107] The radical feminists made quick use of personal contacts and underground networks to publish their writing widely, and also to encourage other women to do so.

TEXTUAL ACTION AND RADICAL FEMINIST LEGACIES

The sheer volume of radical feminist publications, along with the male-exclusion policies enacted in women's liberationist dealings with the mainstream media, created a sprawling, freewheeling, and yet somehow insular print culture in the women's liberation movement. This extensive temporary print culture lasted only a few brief years, roughly from the appearance of *VWLM* and NYRW-published *Notes from the First Year* in 1968 until the gradual publication of radical feminist works by mainstream publishing houses in the early 1970s. Part of the changing textual weather had to do with increased factionalization within the radical movement, factionalization that pushed (as Echols points out) The Feminists and Cell 16 toward cultural feminism and the NYRF toward liberal feminism; dissensus in radical feminist circles about issues of class and elitism had also caused the political withdrawal of movement pioneers such as Firestone.[108] Echols writes that in many ways, radical feminism had planted the seeds of its own demise, since, notwithstanding its opposition to purely personal solutions, "its frequent conflation of the personal and the political made it easy for the cultural feminist commitment to personal transformation or the liberal feminist concern with self-improvement to be defined as political."[109] Part of the change, too, had to do with the necessary refocusing of feminist groups; the editors of *Notes from the Third Year* (December 1971), for example, note that feminist action changes course in 1970, in that the year "has seen fewer manifestoes and more work on specific issues such as prostitution, women's literature, rape, and lesbianism. It has been a period of intensive rather than extensive analysis."[110] To be sure, the phenomena of factionalization and independent feminist projects are related; any movement that has a tenuous national network can only rely on its seeming coherence for so long.

Undoubtedly, however, part of the change was due to the feminists' increasing discomfort with fluid textuality, a discomfort that led activists to seek textual control in the form of individual authorship and copyright. Carden writes that one change, "symbolic of Women's Liberation's partial return to the establishment," is that women's liberationists had begun to question the "practice of reprinting articles without attention to copyright or sometimes even authorship attribution."[111] In fact, as Freeman points out, wider dissemination of radical feminists' ideas was not always in the best interests of the feminists themselves; she writes that one of the early clashes between the women's liberation movement and the larger radical movement happened when the New England Free Press started reprinting uncopyrighted feminist pamphlets at low prices. According to Freeman, while the action "made these materials available to a greater public, it undercut the financial base of the newsletter, which was not highly appreciated."[112] Indeed, trying to finance publications became more of an issue for the radical feminists as their readership increased at the same time that major publishing houses had begun to compete with them for their audience; in 1970 alone, for example, Bantam published Firestone's *The Dialectic of Sex* and Doubleday published Millett's fully fleshed-out *Sexual Politics*, which quickly received mainstream kudos as both a Book-of-the-Month Club selection and a member of the *New York Times* "best books of the year" list. In the same year, Random House published Morgan's *Sisterhood is Powerful*, an edited collection that seemed to make smaller collections like the *Notes* series redundant. All three books became bestsellers.

Morgan herself writes that the process of creating *Sisterhood is Powerful* was a transformative experience that drew her closer to radical feminism and its emphasis on sexism as the primary "-ism" with which to contend; she writes that the anthology "transformed my own views at least as much as it has those of other women, thousands of whom have told me it wrought drastic shifts in their attitudes and in their daily realities."[113] This transformation through text—especially when that text came as a necessary part of an earlier transformation, namely consciousness-raising—seems key to an understanding of how radical feminism operated in the late 1960s, and how it faded by the early 1970s. Like explanations of the beginnings of the radical feminist movement, explanations of its demise seek some cause-effect narrative. Clearly, however, there are a number of reasons for radical feminism disappearing into history, including factionalization of the movement, a refocusing of priorities as feminists were greeted with the more-conservative 1970s, and, perhaps most tellingly, the redefinition of radical feminist principles in order to reinforce a cultural feminist agenda. Echols writes that while:

> the radical feminist movement as a whole was social construction-
> ist . . . the tendency of some radical feminists to blame maleness
> rather than power relations not only encouraged essentialism, but
> also helped shift the focus away from confronting men to building a
> female counterculture as a refuge from contaminating maleness.[114]

It is this nonconfrontational, isolationalist impulse in the histories of feminism and composition that I find particularly troubling. As we have attempted to create a counterculture within composition that valorizes "women's ways of knowing" as a refuge from current-traditional (read: male) pedagogy, we have based that counterculture on our own misconceptions about consciousness and text in the second-wave feminist movement. Long before our contemporary debates about essentialism, radical feminist groups questioned both what it was to *be* a woman and to *perform* womanhood, and a key part of that questioning took the form of very public, very contentious texts—each of which might counter our assumptions about just what typifies "women's writing."

3

FROM MANIFESTO TO MODEM

THERE ARE MANY PARALLELS to be drawn between the youth counterculture of the late 1960s and today's cyberculture, not the least of which is the radical feminist sense of textuality that arises sometimes out of, sometimes in response to, and sometimes in direct contradiction to, larger political moments. Like the underground network of publication that the radical feminists made use of in the late 1960s, the Internet provides the means to hook up feminists nationally and internationally. Unlike the 1960s network, however, the Internet itself exists as a writing technology, one that constructs its texts and their means of dissemination simultaneously. In this liminal space between production and reception, construction and reconstruction, feminists online work in a variety of ways: through listservs, Usenet newsgroups, Web databases, and various other publications. In this chapter, I focus on the "publicly authored" Internet spaces on the World Wide Web (databases, e-zines, and resource sites); specifically, I focus on the heterotopic spaces of Mimi Nguyen's *Exoticize This!* (formerly *Exoticize My Fist*) and Susana L. Gallardo's *Making Face, Making Soul: A Chicana Feminist Homepage*. The publicly transgressive discourses of women online are perhaps most apparent on Web sites such as these, Web sites that invoke a textual identity that becomes increasingly ambiguous as readers contribute texts, sign guestbooks, and provide information to other readers.

It is not my intention, however, to suggest that these spaces exist as sites of the feminist vanguard online, any more than 1960s manifestos existed as a "purer" feminism than the collectives that produced them. Rather, I wish to explore how these generative texts negotiate the odd interplay of fixity and fluidity online, an interplay that at once suggests both the presence of a coherent feminist community-through-text and the inadequacy of coherence as a principle of women's textuality or women's history. The negotiation of the spaces between individual texts and collective networks, in the case of radical feminists and feminists online, creates a temporary stability of purpose and identification. In the case of feminist texts online, this negotiation is made eminently possible through the fluidity of hypertext as a medium. That is, the Internet makes visible the interplay of fixity and fluidity that is part of radical feminist textuality; likewise, the emphasis on a personal, persuasive text within an ambiguously public structure parallels the textual subjectivity of the radical feminists. These feminist Web sites and others serve as active examples of the negotiation of the space between insider and outsider, fixed text and fluid network (and vice versa), and reader and writer.

This negotiation of "between," or liminal, spaces forms a key component of radical feminist textuality, as does the assumption that the texts are necessary; the sense is that if the named creator of the Web site had not created the site, one of the readers just might have. The editors of *Wench*, for example, write that "[too] few voices speak about the lives and concerns of women; if you have something to say (and who doesn't?), we urge you to say it here."[1] Similarly, Nguyen explains the presence of her Web site thus:

> I should explain why I—an already burdened feminist graduate student with multiple 'zines, articles, and other media projects in both development and production—felt inordinately compelled to pick up the gauntlet and tackle this Xenian task (yes, I am a rabid Xena fan!): I got *annoyed*. That is, I got *exceedingly* irritated trying to find rad Asian/American women's work on the Web and figured everybody else must be sick of it too. So much for the Web's "liberating" p.r.: typing "asian women" into search engines will get you about twelve million porno sites.
>
> . . . This is a feminist site. This is an Asian American site. This is an Asian American feminist site. And, as far as I know, it's the only Asian American feminist resource site on the Internet.[2]

Nguyen's express invocation of difference and identity within the context of a network of texts serves as a telling example of textual possibility online.

Just as radical feminists and online feminists emphasize the necessity of text, they emphasize the necessity of action. That is, feminist text and action are similarly ambiguous in their conditions of creation, but regardless of those conditions, they must come to be. As the unnamed author of the "Perfect Woman Rant" at the now-defunct *GiRLRiGHtS!* states:

> You don't have to cause riots or devote yr *[sic]* life to resisting in order to contribute. THE RESPONSIBILITY DOESN'T LIE ON ANY ONE WOMAN'S SHOULDERS, BUT IT IS IN ALL OF OUR HANDS. Alltogether *[sic]*, we can change all of this, every little bit helps . . . Realize, if you resist in a quiet, even casual way, it adds up. Not only will we create a resistance strong enough to balance the presently unequal force exerted on us, but we will also create a resistance so strong that no matter what force is exerted on us, just like the earth, we will be strong enough to match it . . .[3]

Or, as Nguyen writes, "*exoticize this!* is a practical combination of a 'do it yourself' ethic—learned from punk and riot grrrl—and years of feminist and leftist activism and theorizing."[4] Nguyen's emphasis on the active potential of the combinant space between different discourses mirrors that of the radical feminists, and it is this liminal space, I argue, that serves as a site for active and critical textual agency.

The online interplay of fixity, fluidity, text, and identity has much to do with the particular textual ambiguities of online discourse, particularly as evidenced in the preferred medium of hypertext. Hypertext, broadly put, is "the dynamic interconnection of a set of symbolic elements."[5] Hypertext documents are composed of nodes of information linked to each other in multiple ways; there is not necessarily a predetermined top-to-bottom order to the nodes, and indeed one of the terms frequently used to describe hypertextual structure is "horizontal" as opposed to the "top-down" or "vertical" structure of a traditional print text. As hypertext readers choose to follow one path or another in a hypertext—as they read different nodes, that is—they move through a web of information that has no top or bottom, no node that is (organizationally speaking) more important than another. In *Writing*

Space: The Computer, Hypertext, and the Remediation of Print, Jay David
Bolter states that since hypertext "has no canonical order," it facilitates
the reader's ability to construct multiple, equally appropriate, equally
convincing readings of a text; networked text "has no univocal sense; it
is a multiplicity without the imposition of a principle of domination."[6]
Similarly, Stuart Moulthrop and Nancy Kaplan write that as the defining technology of text changes, so too do the conditions of creativity
and interpretation. That is, they write, while print technology demands
"singular and definitive discourse—the production of a literature
devoted to property, hierarchy, and a banking model of culture," hypertext technology "emphasizes cooperation and community" and "invali-
dates priority and singularity."[7] In any event, the reader's part in constructing *any* text is made visible in hypertext, simply because as the
reader navigates hypertext in any of a variety of ways, s/he creates a
unique text through that navigation. Michael Joyce, in one of perhaps
the more well-known discussions of hypertext, draws a distinction
between *exploratory* hypertexts, "closed" instrumental documents such
as training manuals that have a set path through them, and *constructive*
hypertexts, which are "open" texts that require their readers "to create,
to change, and to recover particular encounters" within the developing
text, encounters that "are versions of what they are becoming."[8]

As Johndan Johnson-Eilola notes, "hyperreading" is not itself simply a phenomenon of Internet culture. That is, he writes, print-based
activities "such as reading cross-references in encyclopedias, citations
and footnotes in scholarly works, and the alphabetized names linked to
numbers in a phone book correspond, in a limited way, to the essential
idea behind hypertext."[9] While most writers acknowledge that some
print texts can function hypertextually, however, the term is usually
reserved for a specific type of computer- and/or Internet-based writing.
Hypertext is an openly referential text, and the technology of the Internet, which provides at least theoretically unlimited possibilities for textual *bricolage,* seems particularly suited to this referentiality; as George
Landow and Paul Delany notoriously point out, hypertext is an "embar-
rassingly literal embodiment" of postmodern ideas of textuality.[10]

In *Nostalgic Angels: Rearticulating Hypertext Writing,* Johnson-
Eilola agrees with Landow and Delany, writing that many critics have
argued that "the value placed on nonlinearity, multiplicity, loss of
authorial control, and the association of elements in complex webs
characterizes both hypertext and postmodernism";[11] elsewhere, he

writes that hypertext "can make visible the operations and effects of powerful modern theories of reading and writing—postmodernism and poststructuralism, reader-response criticism and critical literacy, and collaborative learning and social construction theory."[12] On the other hand, Michael Dertouzos, the director of MIT's Laboratory for Computer Science, links hypertext to a laissez-faire textual network, a site in which people "can engage in the useful buying, selling, and free exchange of information with one another."[13] Hypertext has thus proven to be an extremely flexible concept, for better or worse, in the sense that writers from a variety of seemingly incompatible ideological standpoints describe its possibilities with great enthusiasm.

Feminists have claimed hypertext's malleability for their own, drawing connections between the constructive, unhierarchical "web" of the Internet and the "web-thinking" that marks women's moral development, at least according to feminist scholarship drawing from the work of Carol Gilligan; liberal feminists emphasize the egalitarian potential of the Internet, which might provide everyone a seat at the cyber-table.[14] It is this emphasis on cultural and liberal feminist values that has steered feminist compositionist inquiry; feminist compositionists address issues of gendered interaction and computer access rather than the seemingly neutral ground of the World Wide Web itself. If the World Wide Web is indeed a "natural" fit for women, an antihierarchy with great egalitarian potential, then we should focus on how to get *more* women there, or so the argument goes. However, it is less the Internet's *egalitarian* potential than its *subversive* potential that may hold the most promise for feminists in general. As Johnson-Eilola argues, hypertext "forefronts the interaction between social and technological issues in a way not normally seen—or not normally discussed—in the use of print-based, linear texts."[15] This emphasis on the situatedness of text, technology, and subjectivity, as well as the rejection of a hierarchical information structure, can make the World Wide Web a particularly rich site for feminist action, particularly the ambiguous yet purposeful collaboration—a type of "collaborative interruption," that is—that was the hallmark of radical feminism.

SEPARATIST CYBERSPACE

The cultural feminist interest in "women's space" and the liberal feminist emphasis on equity within existing structures has led to an intensive but limited examination of women and technology in composition. That is, feminist compositionists have focused on women's interactive styles in online "conversations" that take place in listservs and MOOs, and also on the community-building capacity that such textual spaces offer. Compositionists such as Cynthia Selfe, Gail Hawisher, Patricia Sullivan, and Mary J. Flores have explored topics such as women-only listservs, computer-conferencing software, the politics of particular computer interfaces, and interactional patterns of women and men online. That is, compositionists examine different online spaces to explore how women interact (and if they do not interact, *why* they do not) but spend less time examining the texts created by women outside the confines of "women's ways of knowing." Unless women's textual action appears to reflect this sense of woman-as-webmaker, cultural and liberal feminist radar does not register it as noteworthy action; thus, there is much discussion of women's listservs, and scant discussion of women's Web sites, which may not demand the immediate interaction of online conversation. As this discussion is limited, so too is its relevance to those outside the fold. The online women's counterculture may be a *needed* refuge, but it does not help us move feminist theory out of separatist cyberspace and into less utopian spaces such as the writing classroom.

I do not mean to suggest that the current conversation about women and technology is an idle one. The types of feminist action proposed and often carried out by feminist compositionists are cultural/liberal feminist actions; discussions of equity and equal access often lead to salutary attempts to change the material conditions of the classroom or the discursive conditions of cyberspace.[16] Even more promising are discussions of identity and network such as the one in Hawisher and Selfe's "Inventing Postmodern Identities: Hybrid and Transgressive Literacy Practices on the Web." In this work, Hawisher and Selfe explore "the ambiguities and contradictions associated with online identity formation, literacy practices, and globalization."[17] Specifically, they look at several international feminist Web sites and how those online feminists "use online literacy practices to transgress against conventional national boundaries, to achieve multiple goals, and to construct cyborgian, hybrid identities in the process of practicing online literacies."[18] It is thus not my purpose here to offer a fully radical reading of women's listserv and network activity *per se;* rather, it is to note that the types of studies conducted (with notable exceptions such as Hawisher and Selfe's) tend to be written from cultural and liberal feminist standpoints. Thus, the questions about women's activity seem to arise "naturally" from feminist theorizing; the ideology and the space are neatly complementary.

The scholarly conversation about women, computers, and composition, then, like the scholarly conversation about women and composition in general, draws much of its energy from the work of feminist developmental psychologists, and thus tends to reflect cultural and liberal feminist ideologies. Many scholars use the work of Gilligan and of the Belenky collaborative in order to examine how women's styles of verbal interaction might keep them from fully reaping the benefits of cyberspace. Flores, for example, advocates computer conferencing that takes as its guide the Belenky collaborative's conception of "constructed knowledge," which integrates personal and public voices and allows students to "participate fully in their educations, as they are able to articulate what they have learned through experience and make connections with the knowledge and experiences of others."[19] Citing Freire's critique of the "banking method" of education, in which students are the passive depositories of received knowledge, Flores writes that our current methods of network use demand women's passivity; in the interests of efficient information disbursal, we "render a portion of our students silent."[20]

Billie J. Wahlstrom relies on a similar interpretation of the work of Gilligan and of the Belenky collaborative in "Communication and Technology: Defining a Feminist Presence in Research and Practice." Wahlstrom writes that feminist theory can "augment" current theoretical discussions of technology; it can also "uncover constraints inherent in hardware and software by revealing that technology is gendered."[21] According to Wahlstrom, such constraints come from computer programmers' ignorance of "women's ways of knowing," and the results of such ignorance have been "programs appealing more to men than to women."[22] To remove these constraints, she argues, we must analyze computer networks from a feminist standpoint. While Wahlstrom does not specify *which* feminist standpoint she believes to be the most helpful—and in fact, standpoints are necessarily rhetorical in that they demand a fluidity of position—it is clear that her argument derives from a cultural and liberal feminist ideology. She writes that feminist analysis:

> critiques technology and its uses, suggesting alternatives that are democratizing and equalizing. It gives us a glimpse of what technology

might be if it were designed for and used in support of women. Because we have other silenced groups in our classes in addition to women, feminist analysis provides a vantage point from which we can imagine applications of technology that enfranchise marginal and oppressed groups.[23]

According to Wahlstrom, then, feminist analyses that take into account these ways of knowing would make the writing classroom more equitable; it is thus that Wahlstrom ties together the work of the Belenky collaborative—so amenable to cultural feminist appropriation—and the historical goals of liberal feminism.

Perhaps one of the stronger voices in the discussion of women and technology is Selfe, who identifies her position as explicitly liberal feminist in "Technology in the English Classroom."[24] Selfe writes that liberal feminism shares with radical and Marxist feminism "the recognition that women (and other minorities) have traditionally been and continue to be devalued, oppressed, and silenced, but it recognizes the possibility of modifying existing political, social, and economic structures to promote and support equity in opportunity."[25] Further, she claims, the more we develop "reduced risk" communication environments like computer conferencing, the more we can offer "traditionally silenced and marginalized students the opportunity to find a voice and to use it effectively in group discussions and conversations."[26]

In her essay, Selfe points specifically to liberal feminist theory as an "alternative vision" of computers in the classroom, a vision of equal access and opportunity. She writes that computer networks "can, in a feminist sense, invite more people into active engagements with, and conversations about, texts and encourage them to participate in different, and perhaps more egalitarian, ways than might be possible using more traditional media."[27] In her discussion of the egalitarian potential of computer networks, Selfe writes that given the right hardware, software, and money to make them work, "computer networks can make it possible for individual writers and readers who have been prevented from entering our academic conversations in the past to become central contributors."[28] The key to developing reduced risk environments, then, at least according to Selfe, is connectivity; she writes that while "connection" is central to a feminist pedagogy, it is not the case that computers have automatically made connection a priority. Citing administrative funding of stand-alone computer systems (and of computers instead of software or necessary cables), Selfe argues that "our current educational computer systems are characterized by communication problems rather than communication exchange."[29] Thus, Selfe's approach to technology seeks to change the material and discursive conditions of marginalized people within the computer- and network-facilitated writing classroom.

While scholars such as Wahlstrom and Selfe offer liberal feminist positions on the potential for computers to make the writing classroom more equitable for *all* marginalized groups, other scholars focus more on the cultural feminist ideal of women's space, a counterculture refuge from the aggressive public world of the Internet, which is, for these scholars, gendered male. In "Women on the Networks: Searching for E-Spaces of Their Own," for example, Hawisher and Sullivan examine a women's "e-space," in this case a women-only listserv, in order to "provide a basis for further discussion of how women activists might transform e-spaces into sites for productive feminist change."[30] Electronic networks, they write, are "neither egalitarian utopias nor sites devoid of power and influence for women" but can "offer women a way into the male-dominated computer culture."[31] Hawisher and Sullivan argue that many feminist studies of women's interactions online tend to portray those women as victims. They write:

> [Recent] studies of women and technology have begun to question the adequacy of egalitarian narratives for describing e-space. . . . Because of the attractiveness of the egalitarian narrative and the persuasiveness of the research that supports it, feminists have needed powerful stories of gender deception, violence, and harassment to counter prevailing notions about the utopian possibilities of e-space.[32]

Hawisher and Sullivan studied woman@waytoofast, a listserv created specifically for their project. The subjects of their study were women academics, ranging in rank from full professor to graduate student. Participants not only contributed to the listserv, but also completed three interviews about their experiences online, including both their experience in woman@waytoofast and their experiences in other online forums.

Hawisher and Sullivan write that the listserv participants "wrote frequently of their desire for a space of their own (and time to spend there). . . . They longed for e-spaces arranged to their liking."[33] The authors emphasize, however, that woman@waytoofast itself was not an attempt to construct a utopian e-space; rather, it served as a site in which "a group of women in composition studies [could] discuss how they would like an e-space constructed" and also "model the kinds of values and actions they might expect of e-space participants."[34] Both the participants who wanted online spaces to be more nurturing and those who wanted those spaces to be more efficient had been disappointed with their experiences online, citing instances of exclusion and attack on the one hand, and superficiality of discussion on the other.[35] Hawisher and Sullivan describe their subjects' utopian visions as visions of a "shelter" and a "heterotopia of crisis," and write that "The welcoming atmosphere, the effort to hear everyone's words, the empathy for those who have been battered in other online forums are all characteristics of an e-space that shelters and supports."[36]

This vision of a sheltering and separate discursive space for women often comes in response to online harassment in listservs, newsgroups, and chatrooms—the highly interactive genres of Internet text. Frequently, that vision is accompanied by the creation of separatist spaces such as women-only listservs (such as Riot Grrls) and moderated newsgroups like soc.women.lesbian-and-bi, whose moderators write that they will not accept posts from men in "introductions" or "looking for friends" categories.[37] Further, they write:

Posts from men will be evaluated under the following rules:

1. Posts conveying information that is factual, analytical, or literary will be relevant if the same post from a woman would be relevant.
2. Posts conveying opinion or experience will be posted if the opinion or experience would seem to be useful to lesbian and bi women, which usually is the case where the opinion or experience is sufficiently gender-neutral as to offer women some insight into the matter being discussed. . . . Men are not allowed to post self-introductions or "looking for friends" messages.[38]

Riot Grrls, as Stephanie Brail writes, is a female-only listserv begun after a particularly nasty round of abuse in the Usenet group alt.zines;[39] a group of women created the female-only listserv Systers after similar abuse in the Usenet group soc.women.[40] In "We Are Geeks, and We Are Not Guys: The Systers Mailing List," L. Jean Camp writes that all too often, "when women try to create spaces to define ourselves, we are drowned out by the voices of men who cannot sit quietly and listen, but need to bring themselves into the discussion."[41] An antidote to the overpowering cyber-voices of men, she argues, is a women-only listserv, a "room of our own" in which women interact in "nurturing communion."[42]

Regardless of whether Camp's glowing account of the Systers list-serv is entirely accurate, she does point to several collaborative actions that arise from the listserv, including a protest of Mattel's 1993 math-phobic Barbie doll (in 1993, Mattel released "Talking Barbie," who said, among other things "Math is hard"; Camp reports that the Systers mailing list organized a complaint-letter-writing campaign to Mattel, and that national attention to the complaints forced Mattel to recall the Barbie).[43] Camp concludes, much as radical women did in the late 1960s, that women-centered discussion groups are only one step toward liberation; she writes that "we cannot live in a sanctuary, regardless of the temptation. It is important to go back out into the public debate and remain visible, if for no other reason than to ensure that no woman is left truly isolated."[44] Similarly, Brail writes that it is important that women take action; the action she suggests, however, is to avoid the rough-and-tumble of mixed-sex online forums:

> The more of us that speak up, the more of us that exist online, the harder it will be to silence us. Perhaps there are places that we won't want to go to—if a place offends us, perhaps we should just stay away—but instead of withdrawing totally from the online world, with all its riches and opportunities, we can form our own networks, online support groups, and places to speak.[45]

Finally, like Camp and Brail, Hawisher and Sullivan also note the difficulty in defining just what constitutes feminist action in an online environment, writing that the same spaces that serve as personal forums can also "function as spaces for political action."[46]

The difficulty that these authors see—and the tension between Brail's advocacy of "speaking up" and her suggestion that women avoid uncomfortable Internet spaces—is the difficulty of advocating radical change at the same time one espouses a liberal philosophy. There is a tension in occupying the seemingly contradictory positions of radical and reformist. Even Selfe has to put aside her advocacy of the equitable classroom when she discusses direct action; she writes:

influenced by feminist theory, we would also want to ensure that increased participation on computer networks or within a computer-supported classroom can, in turn, encourage new, different, even revolutionary *patterns* of information exchange and conversations—those that allow individuals with traditionally marginal relationships to an academic discourse community to bring themselves to the center of that community's exchanges.[47]

What Selfe advocates here, rather than the gradual equalization of power through networking, is the development of "revolutionary" patterns and the inversion of margin/ center relations. This position seems to contradict Selfe's expressed sense of liberal feminism, but in fact it merely points to the tension inherent in any liberal call to action, and particularly a liberal call for *women's* action.

It is not necessarily the case that the Web and women's thinking go hand in hand. Neither is it the case that computers are solely the domain of phallocentric thought. Rather, there is a tension between a structure that these feminists have gendered feminine (the Internet) working with technology that they have gendered masculine (computers). Karen Coyle, for example, draws distinctions between male and female approaches to technology, writing that men tend to be "fascinated with the machine qua machine" while women tend to want to *use* the machine rather than worship it.[48] In "How Hard Can it Be?" Coyle writes even given these distinctions, we do not often question whether computers really are masculine. Because we are too willing to accept the "masculine" status quo as to what constitutes an actual contribution to Internet culture, we often lose sight of women doing interesting and generative things with computers. Coyle writes that "It takes different eyes to see where women have been and what they have done. . . . If we accept the standard view of a male-dominated computer industry, we will never see the women who are making a contribution."[49]

While Coyle's identification with cultural feminism is clear—she worries that we will ignore the relational, nurturing women in favor of the aggressive male "heroes" online—her statement also has radical potential. What happens if compositionists attempt to look beyond the particular ideology that attempts to gender (in remarkably stereotypical ways) structures and technologies? The cultural and liberal feminist projects of revaluing, reclaiming, and reinforcing women online have left by the wayside other important contributions to activist cyberculture, contributions made invisible through the attachment to "women's ways of computing." As long as the conversation about women and technology focuses on ways to make "the system" work for women, and as long as our definition of "women" derives from cultural feminist valorization of "women's ways"—ways that in no way work with "the system"—feminism in composition itself must stay on the margins. In effect, it becomes a holding cell for theories and practices that, because they cannot be contained *inside* the classroom, have to be contained *outside* the classroom; this containment policy is made particularly clear in the current discussions of women online.

RADICAL TEXTUALITY ONLINE

The Internet can serve as an extremely productive place for feminist compositionists, not because of its purported ties to women's ways of knowing, but because its combination of network and text provides real possibilities for collective textual action, action many of us have tried to facilitate in our students' writing and in our own.[50] It is therefore crucial to ground our studies of the Internet in materialities and histories, especially those histories that can take into account the singular action, the anomalous text. As in the general discussion of the intersections of feminism and composition, the discussion of the intersections of feminism, composition, and *technology* relies on a metaphysical logic of essence and hierarchy to explain the present state of women online. Like the curious absence of radical feminist texts in compositionist histories of women and writing, the absence of radical women's Web spaces in our current conversations points to an ideological inability to account for the singularity of those texts and Web spaces. In the particular case of radical women's sites online, the anomalous emphasis on direct action—and perhaps even public confrontation—creates texts that cannot be recognized as "women's" texts within the discourse of cultural and liberal feminism. These texts do not fit, as Foucault might say, the coherent causal whole that is the teleological history of feminism and composition; they are thus un-historied curiosities, outsider texts made invisible.

The un-historied curiosity that is radical feminist textuality has yet to influence composition studies (and thus writing classrooms) in any substantial way; the particular intersections of liberal and cultural

feminism, feminist developmental psychology, and composition studies removed a sense of critical agency in composition classrooms—
through the reification of the ideas of teacher-as-mother, writing-as-
expression, and classroom-as-nurturing-space. If we wish to restore
this sense of agency, however, radical women's textuality offers much
to us as compositionists and feminists. Radical women's textuality,
whether in cyberspace or print culture, emphasizes the idea of a networked community composed of writerly activists, who work individually and collectively through their texts. In their negotiation of structure and fluidity, radical feminist texts emphasize temporary
positionality and the use of available technologies, much in the same
way as Miller's "textual subject" fictionalizes stability in order to act.

A crucial component of women's Internet sites is their association
with other sites through the use of hypertext links and membership in
"Web rings," which are theme-based, loosely connected clusters of
Web sites, each independently created and linked to the others. As
Nicholas C. Burbules notes, it is important to acknowledge the
rhetoricity of hypertext links, to look critically at the chain of identifi-
cations created through connecting one's site to another's; he writes
that hypertext links are "associative relations that change, redefine, and
enhance or restrict access to the information they comprise."[51] The
concept of enhancing and restricting access through hypertext links is
key to an understanding of how any sort of collective might be created
in cyberspace. Burbules argues that when readers select and follow "any
particular line of association between distinct textual points," they are
by necessity interpreting "the nature of association this link implies."[52]
Like the radical feminists' use of a national textual network, albeit an
underground one, online writers' use of links and Web rings creates a
temporary stability of identification, a fictive coherence that serves as
point from which to work for change. The Internet itself replicates
Freeman's "tenuous network of personal contacts and feminist publications"[53] that held second-wave feminism together.

It is a gross overstatement to claim that there are one-to-one parallels between second-wave feminist manifestos and online feminist
texts, however. It is more the case that there are telling similarities in
the textual cultures that occasion such writing, similarities not based on
an evolutionary history of feminism, human rights agitation, or even
print culture. These texts are ambiguous in their causes, just as hypertext and print are ambiguous in their ideological associations. The

online publications often exhibit a more graphics-intensive, consumer-oriented awareness than did the manifestos from the 1960s; however, that awareness is part of the literacies made available by Web technology, just as the "zaps" of the older texts were part of a temporary literacy of political action. Each textuality demands a bobbing-and-weaving, in-your-face attention to politics and textual form; each makes use of collaborative and often anonymous collective work; each, by virtue of the form of text itself, is decidedly temporary. These temporary and mostly collective texts, whether they hail from the 1960s or the 1990s, express a sense of urgency—the feeling is that the authors created the texts because *somebody* had to do it. Another key similarity in these feminist textualities (separated by over 30 years of changes in theory and technology) is the sense of rhetorical purpose. Overwhelmingly, these feminist e-spaces, like radical feminist publications, demand some action from their readers, even if that action is seemingly no more significant than signing a guestbook or linking to the site itself. The textual imperative is a political imperative, a desire to put ideas into collective action.

This move toward collective action through textuality is perhaps most apparent in activist women's Web sites, which combine the relative permanence of a resource site and archive with the ever-changing association of hypertext links, visitor input, and guest commentary. The radical feminist manifestos of the 1960s signaled not the moment of consciousness, but the moments of public identity—the moments when the consciousness developed in discussion groups made itself manifest in text, as part of a collective organized for social change. In cyberspace, that signaling of identity operates similarly, but the notion of "public identity" becomes increasingly ambiguous as the texts themselves openly invite reader construction, not just through different negotiations of links, but through the use of guestbooks, email contacts, and links to similar pages. It is thus important, when examining these Web sites critically, to look not only for the denotative purpose and associative identity, but for the ambiguities of construction. What are the opportunities for reader participation in and construction of the site? How are the links assembled, and how do they change? Where does textual identity make its presence known, and how and when does that shift?

Part of the difficulty in examining feminist Web sites is that, despite the concern that the Internet is a forbidding climate for women, there is a wealth of sites that identify themselves as "feminist." A cursory search on "feminist" at the yahoo.com search engine <http://www.yahoo.com>, for example, revealed close to 1.5 million "hits." While not all of the hits are feminist sites (in fact, the only thing many of the sites have in common is that the word "feminist" appears somewhere on the site), it is safe to assume that feminist sites could easily number in the hundreds, if not thousands. Not all online feminist publications serve the same purpose, however; neither do they necessarily contribute anything new to feminist textual culture. Many Web sites, for example, function primarily as truncated versions of their print counterparts, neither publishing nor soliciting input to their Web sites. U.S. feminist mainstays *Off Our Backs, Ms.,* and *On the Issues* have their own Web sites (http://www.igc.apc.org/oob/, http://www.Msmagazine.com, and http://www. echonyc.com/~onissues/, respectively), which publish featured articles from the print journal in excerpt or in full, provide current tables of contents, and—perhaps their primary purpose—provide information about how to subscribe or contribute to the print magazine.

Other online feminist publications such as *Wench* <http://www. wench.com> and *Feminista!* <http://www.feminista.com> replicate the look and editorial policies of traditional print publications, but do not have print counterparts. These publications do attempt to take advantage of the textual ambiguities made possible by Internet technology. In their original (1996) "Forward," for example, the *Wench* editors wrote that their online publication was "more fluid" than a print magazine, and that it served as a "gallery of ideas."[54] Despite the fact that the gallery of ideas in *Wench* was a gallery of *essays,* however, the editors wrote that their intent was to publish a variety of textual forms:

> Those ideas will come in as many forms as they do in the real world, from sharply-written articles to angrily-scribbled rants, from complex imagery to simple, unambiguous doodles. While we have a vague idea of the direction we're headed, we look forward to letting the winds take us where they may.[55]

In the years since that intent was made public, however, *Wench* has undergone a substantial editorial revision, writing in 2000 that they have "a new look, new content, an expanded staff and an expanded mission. . . . We've expanded our mission to include topics that are not strictly 'feminist,' but which share some of the same social, personal and political terrain."[56] Even more standard is statement of purpose of *Feminista!*, a publication that "aspires to be an online journal of such quality that we are known regionally, nationally and internationally for our content and networking capacity."[57] For both of these journals, and other Internet publications like them, reader contributions are limited to "submissions" (a telling phrase about publisher/author relations) and letters to the editor. These online journals, regardless of their aspirations to multitudinous textual form and wide networking, function as cyber-translations of print form; there is little contained in these Web sites that could not be contained as well by print technology. In effect, then, these sites function as Joyce's "exploratory" hypertexts, that is, providing "closed" access (and often set pathways) to information in the site.

The Internet also hosts many sites that use new networking capabilities in order to target women as consumers instead of as agents of social change. For example, sites such as *Cybergrrl* <http://www.cybergrrl.com/> claim as their purpose "informing, inspiring and celebrating women," show up as feminist sites on many Internet search engines, and offer women a variety of networking features, such as chatrooms, forums, and pages of informational links. However, the underlying purpose of *Cybergrrl* (a division of Cybergrrl, Inc.) like other commercial sites, is not to effect political change, but to "empower" its corporate sponsors at the expense of its readers. On its "Client Services" page, the writers explain that "Cybergrrl, Inc. is a media and entertainment company specializing in online content, resources, sites and communities for women and girls. . . . We are pioneers in using the Internet as an effective marketing and communication tool."[58] Cybergrrl, Inc., writes that it "has a network of women's Web sites reaching women overall between the ages of 18–45+ and offering sponsors and advertisers unique relationship-building opportunities to reach this loyal and active audience.[59] *Femina*, another division of Cybergrrl, Inc., does marginally better than *Cybergrrl;* in its "About" section, it reports that its purpose is "to provide women with a comprehensive, searchable directory of links to female friendly sites and information on the World Wide Web."[60] However, *Femina*, like its parent organization, has a commercial community in mind; its community, it tells potential advertisers, is a "highly targeted, highly responsive audience."[61] Other sites that take advantage of the marketing capability of networks in cyberspace include *Bust Magazine* <http://www.bust.com>, which serves as a sort of *Reader's Digest* for the terminally hip post-feminist, and *Peach Berserk Cocktails* <http://www.peachberserk.com/>, a sort of Tank-Girl-Meets-Helen-Gurley-Brown fashion site.

In contrast both to online journals and the overly mercantile sites like Cybergrrl, sites like Nguyen's *Exoticize This!* <http://members.aol. com/Critchicks/>, also known as *Exoticize My Fist!*, involve readers in ongoing constructions of feminist identity. The site and its author make no bones about associative political identity; in her "Original State-ment," the manifesto-like invocation of textual identity, Nguyen writes that she is "(unapologetically) feminist, poststructuralist, [and] leftist," and that those ideologies inform everything on her pages; likewise, she writes, her site is "an Asian American feminist site," and that at the time of her writing, it was "the only Asian American feminist resource site on the Internet."[62] Nguyen writes that her Web site "is in some small way my attempt to create a 'virtual' community for asian american fem-inists—as well as act as a coalition-building tool to create networks with asian feminists—in light of the void. but even more, i'm just one stop-over in a growing chain of awesome feminists period on the Web."[63]

Nguyen has designed *Exoticize This!* specifically as a resource site, and does provide a wealth of themed information pages (themes include "politics + activists," "pop culture," "allies + friends," "queer," and "grrrls + personal pages," among others) containing hypertext links to other Web sites. However, more than just providing access to other places, *Exoticize This!* contains Nguyen's bibliographies, a link to her own e-zine, *worsethanqueer* <http://www. worsethanqueer.com/>, a list of Asian American feminist academics, and an interpretive commen-tary on every link that Nguyen provides. As Nguyen herself writes, the site "will always be under construction."[64] Key to that ongoing con-struction is Nguyen's ongoing solicitation of reader contributions in the form of suggestions and site links.

In her "Original Statement," Nguyen tells her readers why she felt compelled to create an Asian American feminist resource site; in short, she is compelled because of the absence of such sites online. She writes:

> I want substantive and feminist girlie action . . . I want heavy theory mixed in with radical lesbionics, museum art installations and grubby print 'zines, and I want to find them all in one place! As such, this is way more than a link site since I'm having to write whole bibliogra-phies, for instance, all by myself, for amazing women that aren't to be found, it seems, anywhere on the Web.[65]

From the time that Nguyen wrote her "Original Statement" in September 1997 to its most recent update in April 1999, it is clear that a good deal more "amazing women" have surfaced on the Internet, given the number of links Nguyen has compiled. Many of these women's sites, including Nguyen's, existed until very recently as part of the now-defunct "Third World Women Web-Ring," a metacommunity of Web sites linked only by HTML and the loose association of identity created through sharing that Web ring. At its height, the Third World Women Web-Ring indexed 43 Web sites, including Nguyen's, the *Third-World-Women E-Zine* (now at http://www.cyberdiva.org/erniestuff/ezine.html) and FemiNet Korea <http://www.feminet.or.kr/>.

Inspired by Nguyen's work in *Exoticize This!*, Susana L. Gallardo designed and still maintains *Making Face, Making Soul: A Chicana Feminist Homepage* <http://www.chicanas.com>. Referring to herself as the "webjefa," Gallardo writes that:

> *Making Face, Making Soul* is a site by, for, and about Chicanas, meaning women of Mexican descent in the United States. . . . I hope you enjoy visiting and revelling in from *[sic]* the fact that there are tons of us chicanas/latinas/mexicanas out here and that we are doing some pretty wonderful and amazing things, things that don't always get noticed by the media or the history books. From raising healthy children in this crazy world we live in, to being bilingual teachers, to *activistas locas,* chicanas are *kicking ass* and i am proud to be telling about it.[66]

Like Nguyen's Web site, *Making Face, Making Soul* is rich with links to outside Web pages, each one an identification of associations, a textual invocation of identity and purpose. The site includes links to a digital and public art project, the Welfare Warriors Web site, the Frontera News Service, library resources in Chicana/Chicano Studies, and individual Web pages of Chicana artists. Other links keep readers within *Making Face, Making Soul,* serving as gateways to a list of Chicana/Latina academics (which Gallardo writes was inspired directly by Nguyen's list of Asian-American feminist academics) and to a list of "Chicanas Chingonas," who are "Chicanas and Latinas who . . . offer us insight and vision as they critique, reform, and incite change through different forms of social, political, and educational activism."[67] Gallardo's site is even more open to public construction than Nguyen's; she publishes guest columns by other Chicanas, actively solicits contributions to her list of Chingonas, and has an extensive guestbook, full of requests for information (which is provided, in turn, by other guestbook signers) and posts about the importance of *Making Face, Making Soul.*

Guestbook activity, while seemingly inconsequential, may sometimes be the text that keeps a Web site functional, and it is in this sense that the reader-construction possibilities of Internet textuality may realize their radical potential. A case in point is the mostly defunct—although currently in the process of relaunching—Web site of the Canadian Women Internet Association (CWIA) <http://www.her-place.org/>. The site's creators certainly intended to facilitate a feminist community online, writing that the CWIA site:

> serves as a resource centre and meeting place for Canadian women. Our Information Resource Centre contains hundreds of links to sites relevant to women, with a special focus on Canadian content. Our interactive guestbook allows you to meet other women or speak your mind on the Web. We also have mailing lists that we use to stay in touch with each other, and to express our many unique ideas and perceptions of the world. Don't be shy to check us out. We look forward to hearing from you![68]

The site offers a space for posting jobs and resumes, links to e-zines, an outdated calendar of upcoming events, a variety of information-link pages on issues including sexuality, spirituality, sisterhood, and motherhood, and an exhaustive collection of women's studies links. The CWIA also sponsors a virtual protest—an annual "candlelight vigil" to raise awareness of violence against women, in response to the December 6, 1989 murder of 14 women (accused by the gunman of being "feminists") at Montreal's Ecole Polytechnique. Participants can download a JPEG image of a candle, put it on their own Web site, and link back to the CWIA page on violence against women, which in turn links to a variety of online resources and articles on the subject. Slight investigation reveals, however, that the CWIA itself no longer has a viable presence on its own site; on the "About Us" page, there is a note stating that the page has been taken down while the group restructures its aims; the note is from 1997.

Regardless of the absence of any recent "official" input from the CWIA, however, the site itself is still active—for now; the guestbook continues to receive posts, and the writers of the posts continue to respond to one another, providing introductions, information about Web site construction, links to other feminist Web sites, and information about upcoming events around Canada. One of the most recent posts is an offer of help to CWIA; Sheila Eastman writes "Your site is a little frustrating to me—no direct contact and it hasn't been updated since Sept. 1997?? Do you need some help with updating?? I would be please [sic] to assist."[69] It is thus that the initial goals of the Web site's creators— to provide resources and meeting places for feminists online—continue to be met, making the Web site itself a truly generative text, one that continues to be read and written even in the absence of its authors.

   The 3rd WWWave: Feminism for a New Millennium <http://www.io. com/~wwwave/> is a feminist Web site that most closely resembles the radical feminist manifestos of the late 1960s. The text begins with an invocation of identity that distinguishes the 3rd-WWWavers from other feminists; "We are a group of women who feel passionately about women's issues, and we decided to put up a site that would reflect the unique view of women's issues and feminism in the generation of women who came of age in the 80's."[70] Further, the 3rd-WWWavers claim that they "are putting a new face on feminism, taking it beyond the women's movement that [their] mothers participated in, bringing it back to the lives of real women who juggle jobs, kids, money, and personal freedom in a frenzied world."[71] The text goes on to list specific gender-based grievances, most of which could have been plucked directly from the Redstockings' work. Finally, the 3rd-WWWavers write:

We've had enough!

- Enough with the guys who refuse to change their roles to match the changes women have made;
- Enough with the old notion that women are permanent victims who will never succeed against sexism;
- Enough with the women who think feminism is over because a few laws protect us and "we're all equal now";
- Enough with the male standard that puts women at a disadvantage in everyday life ("level playing field"—hah!)[72]

The Web site provides a several different pages on women's history, including links to outside resources such as The National Women's

History Project; a page that talks about growing up female and provides links to information on body image, self-mutilation, and gendered toys; and a page of Web resources, including links to e-zines,
search engines, and women Webmasters ("Women who've done it.").
A "Spotlight" section links randomly to Web pages of or about
"women making a difference"—a group that can include anyone from
a woman magician to a network newscaster to astronaut Shannon
Lucid. Interestingly, the sites spotlighted do not contain a reciprocal
link to *The 3rd WWWave*, raising the question (particularly in the case
of corporate sites like cnn.com) of whether the recipients of the spotlight realize that they have been selected.

Like Nguyen's site, *The 3rd WWWave* is part of a larger network of
sites—in this case, both the Leftgrrls Web ring and the Banned Sites
Web ring—and thus creates a momentary stability for itself through its
associative link to a "public" network. The 3rd-WWWavers duly note
that their pages operate through association and bricolage rather than
unified coherence. "We do not agree about everything," they write, "*and
that's OK*. Feminism was never monolithic, and it never will be. You will
hear several voices on these pages; many articles speak for all of us, but
some just for the authors in the byline. We hope our voices will help you
find your own."[73] As far as its more conventional associations, *The 3rd
WWWave* sits somewhere between the overt mercantilism of *Cybergrrl*
and the leftist rejection of e-capital of *Exoticize This!* Some of its associative identity, then, at least in relation to textual capital, is ambiguous in
ways that that of other feminist Web sites is not. Specifically, the Web site
provides a "Feminist Bookshelf" with lists and reviews of books that readers have found relevant to feminist action, and then links to Amazon.com
so that interested feminists can buy the books. *The 3rd WWWave* gets a
commission on any book sold through such links, and thus supports itself
without resorting to the random banner ads of "free" Web servers such as
Geocities.com and Tripod.com. Its association with Amazon.com adds
an element of textual control to the *3rd WWWave* site, much as the move
toward copyright and paid advertising marked a move away from textual
fluidity in the texts of the late 1960s radical feminists.

Part of the importance of these radical women's Web sites is that
they serve as good examples of writers in a network linking up with
other writers, creating community through text without retreating
from public space. These networked texts openly challenge the seeming hegemony of the Internet, using writing as subversion even while

the sites conform, to greater and lesser degrees, to the textual conventions of their public cultures. Thus, these texts and their authors negotiate the terrain between insider status and outcast. Web authors such as Nguyen and Gallardo *do* know how to write for the Internet and find the network lacking from an insider perspective as well as an outsider perspective.

The negotiation of a dual insider/outsider status informs much of the early work of the radical feminists in the 1960s, especially since many women had learned their political tactics from working inside the male-dominated New Left—working inside the movement, however, meant working outside the circle of power, if one was female. There are other negotiations, as well. Radical feminists mediate between fixed texts and fluid networks, or sometimes between fluid texts and fixed networks; at the same time, they negotiate the space between a textual collective derived from an insistence on the primacy of women's struggle and an ideological resistance to the logic of primacy and coherence. Again, just as the texts of the radical feminists and the Web sites of radical women do not correspond neatly, neither do the disparate negotiations of their creators. The similarities of the *sites* of such negotiations cannot be ignored, however. Radical feminist textual subjectivity exists as a response and a challenge to the networks of text and power that inform it.

The temporary texts emanating from the radical feminist movement of the late 1960s, like many of the Web sites created by radical women in today, can serve as interruptions to narratives of textual capital and control. Internet technology lends itself to temporary literacies much as the mimeograph machine and an underground network of texts did thirty years ago. While current trends in Internet regulation, such as increasing commodification, copyright legislation, and anti-content laws, suggest that the network may soon become inimical to social activism (if it is not so already), it is also the case that print culture has been subjected to the same sorts of regulation in its much longer history. In both print culture and cyberculture, that is, there are possibilities for localized resistance; radical feminist textuality very much takes advantage of those possibilities, through a combination of temporary, flexible texts and the subversive use of existing networks and structures that make those texts public.

What does this textual subjectivity of these Web authors tell us about writing that we didn't know before? Compositionists have long been interested in the pedagogical possibilities of network technologies such as the Internet, devoting much energy to topics like collaborative learning, distance learning, and what it means for students to have the opportunity to publish their work in front of a "real" audience. In addition, such low-end Internet technologies as e-mail, newsgroups, and interactive spaces like MOOs and MUDs have refigured much composition pedagogy and scholarship, if the latest programs from CCCC and the popularity of the annual Computers & Writing Conference are any indication. For feminist compositionists in particular, issues of identity and technology seem to have focused attention on how to create private and separate space in a pervasively public network. I do not think that the importance of the intersections of feminism, composition, and technology has been underestimated. However, if we intend to use those intersections as a means by which to effect meaningful change in both our wired and our unwired classrooms, we have been looking in the wrong places.

4

TEXTUALITY, PERFORMATIVITY, AND NETWORK LITERACIES

THIS CHAPTER TAKES as its starting point the tension, noted by Nguyen, between "liberatory" textuality and material conditions, examining the uneasy fit of feminist and cultural studies approaches to composition, approaches that are too often yoked together in an effort to contain all liberatory pedagogies in the same taxonomic space. In the midst of examining the feminist critique of cultural studies, however, I will also point to certain generative intersections of feminism, composition, and cultural studies. Specifically, I explore what it might mean to enact a performative pedagogy that takes into account the discourses of the classroom at the same time as it values a radical feminist negotiation of the spaces between binaries. A radical feminist attention to text and network provides us with a key example of how to connect liberatory discourse, material conditions, and text.

When Nguyen dismisses the discussion of the Internet's liberatory potential as so much public-relations hype,[1] she points to a key tension in discussions of textuality and pedagogy—namely, that tension between liberatory pedagogies and material conditions. As bell hooks writes, students rightfully expect "knowledge that is meaningful" and also that their teachers "will not offer them information without addressing the connection between what they are learning and their overall life experiences."[2] It is therefore important that any transformative, student-centered pedagogy take into account the diverse and often conflicted discourses of the writing classroom, particularly if that pedagogy professes to be nonracist and nonsexist. While critical pedagogy and cultural studies approaches to composition form two valuable and productive sites for feminist inquiry, that is, the almost knee-jerk affiliation of these different bodies of scholarship elides many questions of difference, equity, and agency. For example, Carmen Luke writes that a key problem for feminists in critical pedagogy is that the discourse of critical pedagogy insists on empowering people for citizenship in a public-sphere democracy, without critiquing "liberal capitalism's fundamental structural separations and politics of sexual division and subjugation."[3] Critical pedagogy, that is, "constructs a masculinist subject which renders its emancipatory agenda for 'gender' theoretically and practically problematic."[4] Feminist critiques of cultural studies, similarly, question the masculinist tradition of that body of work. It is not the case that feminist and other liberatory pedagogies *necessarily* work together. That said, however, feminist and other liberatory pedagogies have much to offer each other, particularly if current feminist work in composition begins to take into account the possibilities of a radical feminist textuality. Radical feminist textuality provides one way into an interactive, engaged, *performative* pedagogy[5] that values students and teachers as textual, writerly subjects.

CRITICAL TEXTUAL AGENCY AND THE ENGAGED CLASSROOM

The radical feminists of the late 1960s and early 1970s, as well as their online counterparts of the 1990s, offer feminist compositionists provocative examples of networked textuality, a discourse dependent on the constant and visible contextualization of self and writing within the discourses of hegemony. Further, this discourse makes visible a local, situated, and *rhetorical* textual agency at the same time as its stapled-together network invokes more global, or public, concerns. Radical feminists and their attention to text demonstrate how the personal intersects the political through a network of text. Further, they show us an actively constructivist attention to political action, in that personal consciousness within a collective leads to collective action, which in turn changes the personal consciousness of each of the collective's members; that is, radical feminist textuality makes visible the interplay between writer and reader, relying only on a rhetoricized stability for moments of understanding and then action.

It is not the case that all radical feminist texts are manifestos, nor that feminist online spaces are the cyber-equivalent of manifestos. Rather, they exist as what Foucault has called "heterotopic spaces," or *lived* spaces rather than utopian spaces; they are slices of time that simultaneously invoke and communicate a culture's values.[6] The radical feminists, with their encouragement of ambiguous and/or collaborative authorship, their insistence on the personal-as-political, and their use of writing to invoke identity, make liberatory discourse and materiality connect through the moment of text. This conception of textual agency is particularly relevant to a discussion of composition as a *written* field rather than a *spoken* field. As Miller points out in her 1989 *Rescuing the Subject: A Critical Introduction to Rhetoric and the Writer*, scholars who seek to situate modern composition studies within the history of rhetoric too often ignore the fact that that history is a history of oratory.

In this book, Miller recasts the history of rhetoric, emphasizing its written aspects rather than its tradition of oratory in order to posit the idea of a "writing subject"; the writing subject, she claims, mediates uniquely "between actual and symbolic linguistic domains in ways that place [the writer] in a separate and hitherto undescribed textual world."[7] Miller advocates a "textual rhetoric" that places writers, not orators or authors, "in a position of agency in a history and theory of discourse."[8] She writes:

> We can . . . explain historically why it remains feasible to investigate the human "writer" without necessarily surrounding that person with the now easily deniable claptrap of inspired, unitary "authorship" that contemporary theorists in other fields have so thoroughly deconstructed. By clarifying our own stance toward the writer and the history relevant to that position, we demonstrate that composition now has a historically mandated explanatory role among other textual studies.[9]

Most notably for my discussion here, Miller resists a teleological, cause/effect approach to history, instead looking thematically at the history of writing-as-rhetoric. Drawing from discussions of writing in Plato, Quintilian, St. Bonaventura, Ramus, and others, she traces the emergence of the writing subject, someone who "fictionalizes" stability, who always writes for the first time, and who engages in a "process liberated from enclosure in either self-referential language or the world of readers."[10] Miller offers an alternative educational tradition based on the history of writing which, she says, emphasizes a shift from authority vested in a person to authority vested in a text; at the same time, Miller writes, the history of writing is a history of increasing intertextuality, an increased complication of the presence of the writer within the text. Miller proposes, then, a "textual" rhetoric, one that "is based not on customary traditions about historical continuity between rhetoric and composition instruction but on placing writing and writers in a position of agency in a history and theory of discourse."[11]

What are the pedagogical consequences of such a rhetoric? An underlying purpose of Miller's historical project is to lay the groundwork for a discussion of the precarious position of student writers. According to Miller, writing instruction makes student discourse something that happens as a private communication between student and teacher (especially when it comes down to grading time) at the same time as it purports to be public writing. In most academic settings, Miller claims, writing students "write what only a teacher reads, but they have often been assigned a task of imitating traditional public, persuasive forms of writing . . . they are asked to shout in the study, to whisper in the Coliseum."[12] Students thus occupy an untenable position; even as their status as writing students marks them as having been passed over by "genius," that attribute of the gifted and inspired writer, they must still write complexly and originally.[13] Miller closes her book with an examination of Mina Shaughnessy's *Errors & Expectations* because, as she writes, "the best place to end is where composition always begins, in the writing of students."[14] Shaughnessy's work makes us acknowledge discourse as discourse; that is, Miller writes, "basic writing shows that to be a complete and forceful person who 'speaks,' and to make a point in writing that is 'clear' to all, is a problematic identity that requires us to fictionalize, not to re-create, stable meanings."[15] The subjectivity of student writers, then, is a particularly textual subjectivity, one that relies on fictionalized stability in order to negotiate the power relations undergirding a writing classroom. It is thus that Miller's view of the textual subject—as a writer who writes from a liminal space in order to negotiate meaning—can inform our own discussions of liberatory pedagogies of writing, particularly as those pedagogies are informed by radical feminist textuality.

The concept of "engaged pedagogy" is key to an understanding of the potential for radical textuality in the writing classroom. The concept, developed by hooks, depends on a view of students and teachers as real people who are cognizant of their situatedness. According to hooks, engaged teachers transgress the boundaries that confine students to assembly-line pedagogy and approach students "with the will and desire to respond to our unique beings, even if the situation does not allow the full emergence of a relationship based on mutual recognition."[16] Engaged pedagogy calls for the creation of classrooms as participatory spaces in which students and teachers connect classroom knowledge with lived experience. hooks writes that engaged pedagogy demands more from its teachers than do conventional critical or feminist pedagogy, because it demands that the teacher be committed actively to his/her own self-actualization.[17] Further, hooks claims, engaged teachers must acknowledge their own situatedness as part of education as a "practice of freedom." She writes that "professors who expect students to share confessional narratives but who are themselves unwilling to share are exercising power in a manner that could be coercive."[18] Engaged pedagogy thus assumes the personal on the part of teacher and student, emphasizing the situatedness of any writer or rhetor; in a similar vein, radical feminism, with its emphasis on collaborative and networked agency for the purposes of social change, emphasizes the personal on the part of its practitioners.

Henry Giroux and Patrick Shannon see similar potential for a committed, situated pedagogy in their exploration of the intersections of cultural studies and critical pedagogy; they write that the fields of cultural studies and critical pedagogy share many ideological and pedagogical practices but rarely speak to each other because of disciplinary boundaries.[19] What lies at the intersection of these fields, they write, is a "performative pedagogy," an approach that corrects what they see as the developing tendency in cultural studies to "reduce the discipline to a methodological reading of texts."[20] Performativity as a pedagogical practice, then, can move cultural studies away from an overly textual focus and toward a critique of material manifestations of power relations. Drawing from Derrida's concept of "performative interpretation," Giroux and Shannon write that a performative pedagogy refuses "to reduce politics to the discursive or representational" and "suggests reclaiming the political as a pedagogical intervention that links cultural texts to the institutional contexts in which they are read."[21] Key to discussions of cultural studies is the notion of the public intellectual, someone who "walks the walk," as it were, by resisting "the academic institutionalization of social criticism."[22] Giroux and Shannon write that public intellectuals must define themselves "not as marginal, avant-garde figures, professionals, or academics acting alone, but as critical citizens whose collective knowledge and actions presuppose specific visions of public life, community, and moral accountability."[23] The figure of the public intellectual, then, has much in common with hooks's engaged teacher (and with engaged students) in that each is cognizant of the discourses and networks of power that create a "personal" life and a "public" one. Each, that is, cultivates an awareness of the ongoing, rhetorical rewriting of one's identity in the context of different social relations, both inside and outside the university.

"Feminist education for critical consciousness," writes hooks, "is rooted in the assumption that knowledge and critical thought done in the classroom should inform our habits of being and ways of living outside the classroom."[24] That is, she continues:

> without the capacity to think critically about our selves and our lives, none of us would be able to move forward, to change, to grow. . . . Engaged pedagogy has been essential to my development as an intellectual, as a teacher/professor because the heart of this approach to learning is critical thinking. Conditions of radical openness exist in any learning situation where students and teachers celebrate their abilities to think critically, to engage in pedagogical praxis.[25]

It is this sort of education that an attention to radical feminist textuality makes possible. The "radical openness" of the personal made political in the context of a network of texts creates rich soil for resistance to the discourse of hegemonic power. The emphasis on personal engagement and collective agency forms a key part of liberatory pedagogies; as Giroux and Shannon note, a crucial part of the democratizing impulse of critical pedagogy is "a conception of the political that is open yet committed, respects specificity without erasing global considerations, and provides new spaces for collaborative work engaged in productive social change."[26] Similarly, Luke insists that the negotiation of local and global concerns can be emancipatory; we need not slip endlessly into postmodern difference and specificity as long as we keep our attention on "historical structures of domination and exploitation."[27] It is thus that radical feminism offers us a conception of agency within the postmodern—not through the separate space of "women's ways of knowing," nor through an uncritical acceptance of critical pedagogies that elide questions of gender and race, but through a historically situated and textually oriented approach to a consciousness of the "personal" and thus to collective and networked action.

CULTURAL STUDIES, PASSING, AND INTERRUPTION AS AGENCY

Cultural studies scholarship and methodology offers much to feminist compositionists, including an explicit attention to the genealogical discourses of history that pervade any discussion of text and subjectivity. Cultural studies provides at the very least, then, a means by which to reclaim the radical feminists in all their singularity. Radical feminists insisted that we pay attention to the political component of the "personal," and also to the "pro-woman argument," which saw women's participation in the discourses of power not as a "natural" complicity but as reaction and resistance to those discourses. When Kreps writes that we cannot "understand woman's so-called 'nature'" without examining the discourses surrounding and constructing her,[28] she calls for an active contextualization of women within their social relations.

The active contextualization of oneself within discourses of power is part of the project of cultural studies, which forms one of the more productive sites for feminist compositionists—and for feminist scholars in general. As hooks notes, cultural studies forms a site in which one can freely transgress boundaries; it is also "a location that enabled students to enter passionately a pedagogical process firmly rooted in education for critical consciousness, a place where they felt recognized and included, where they could unite knowledge learned in classrooms with life outside."[29] Perhaps because of its seemingly easy fit with student-centered pedagogies, cultural studies also proves to be a generative site for compositionists in general. In "Composition Studies and Cultural Studies: Collapsing Boundaries," for example, James Berlin offers a historical analysis of the intersections of composition studies and cultural studies to show that the endeavors of both fields are "mutually enriching."[30] Berlin looks optimistically toward projects in composition studies that parallel those in cultural studies, particularly projects that "signal the emergence of a social epistemic rhetoric, a rhetoric that considers signifying practices in relation to the ideological formation of the self within a context of economics, politics, and power."[31]

Berlin praises in particular recent projects that examine the "relation between the composition class and critical theory."[32] This examination is by no means an easy one; Berlin writes:

> Asking a group of students to interrogate the conventions of the privileged social class they are working hard to enter—the class to which the teachers already comfortably belong—is not an easy task, and the process may involve discomfort for teachers and students alike. To refuse to engage the ideological dimensions of "ordinary discourse," however, is to acquiesce to injustices that underwrite class, race, gender, age, and other invidious distinctions.[33]

Elsewhere, Diana George and Diana Shoos offer a similar argument (and warning), writing that composition studies can learn much from cultural studies, since both fields have as their goals their students' critical consciousnesses. Composition classes, according to George and Shoos, call upon students "to write about what they remember, what they are currently experiencing, and what they discover through observation, research, and critique."[34] Like Berlin, George and Shoos write that the facilitation of critical consciousness can be an arduous pedagogical task:

> We have claimed that we do not necessarily want students to adopt our point of view or to reject outright the values of the dominant ideology. Yet, in promoting resistance, we run the risk that students will attack the things we love or embrace the things we hate. This is no small concern, especially given the inequitable power relationship between students and instructors, one which is consolidated by the institutional framework of the university. Perhaps the most critical problem becomes how we live up to the ideals of a liberatory pedagogy like Freire's, how we resist falling into old patterns of authority when those are the ones most available to us.[35]

The key problem, alluded to by George and Shoos, is that quite often the only position that liberatory pedagogies offer students is one of resistance, as if differences could be elided in that way to produce a universal rejection of discourses of power. It is in this sense that these approaches are curiously utopian in their depiction of difference; what about students who reject, for whatever reason, our notion of resistance? What about those who subscribe to the tenets of the dominant discourse? Most important to our discussion here, what about students—and teachers—whose very membership in a community of resistance is at question?

Like Giroux and Shannon, Pamela Caughie advocates a performative pedagogy to get at the knotty questions of identity and power in the classroom; however, she problematizes the notion of a public intellectual, arguing against the invocation of citizenship in a resistant, public, "radical democracy" as something that which can move us past difference. Specifically, she writes that the discourses that structure classroom dynamics put into question "any expectation that teaching will end in a shared understanding or reach some kind of consensus."[36] Any pedagogy that attempts to establish consensus, writes Caughie, must at the same time "provide a mechanism for self-consciously displacing the authority of that position."[37] According to Caughie, it is the dual task of taking authority and displacing it that places feminists in cultural studies in a double-bind; to take on power in a classroom, even resistant power, is to position oneself other than where one professes to be—to "pass," in other words.[38] Caughie argues that all feminists must understand the relation of passing to pedagogy in order to participate in a cultural studies program. The double-bind of actual position versus professed position is, however, not specific to feminists; all those who profess cultural studies "pass" and in fact may enact "passing as pedagogy," which is "the way others are elided in the very process of claiming to include them, the way conflicts are not aired at the same time they are acknowledged as essential."[39] According to Caughie, passing as pedagogy is only negative as long as it remains unconscious; as a performative pedagogy, however, a deconstructive approach to passing would subvert power relations at the same time as it invoked them. Feminists and cultural studies scholars share the purpose of critiquing the politics of representation within the dominant culture, Caughie continues; it is thus "all the more imperative that feminists force cultural studies to confront directly the disparity in representation within the university itself, from curriculum to personnel."[40]

As Nedra Reynolds points out, however, cultural studies (and cultural studies in composition) is marked as "a distinctly male enterprise" that "still rests on a canon of works by men."[41] Thus, she writes, "following through on the implications of feminist agency means . . . finding specific conversations in composition studies where it is necessary to interrupt a troubling inattention to the influence of feminist theory and politics. . . ."[42] It is in the service of this interruption that Reynolds offers her own critique of cultural studies' white, male tradition. Reynolds sees the issue of *agency* as that which connects feminism and composition studies, and explores "interruption" as a means to agency for women writers. "Agency," she writes, "is not simply about finding one's own voice but also about intervening in discourses of the everyday and cultivating rhetorical tactics that make interruption and resistance an important part of any conversation."[43] Lisa R. Langstraat, too, notes that while cultural studies scholarship has much to offer feminists in composition, that scholarship is "often informed by a phallocentricity which undermines its liberatory possibilities, reinscribes a split between masculine and feminine epistemologies, and ultimately leaves intact the very oppressive discursive borders that cultural studies claims to revise."[44] Langstraat points to the "hypermasculinity" of cultural studies' position in relation to feminized mass culture, writing that by occupying that position, cultural studies compositionists often construct students as "passive receptacles of popular culture, a construction that reinforces a split between the authority of critical scholar/teachers and that of distracted fan/students."[45] Langstraat rightly notes that the position of students in a cultural studies classroom can too often be constructed as the unconscious, unknown Other to the teacher as agent; there is no room for an engaged pedagogy in such a classroom, for neither student nor teacher exist as beings with lived experiences that inform classroom discourse.

What these writers and others advocate are transformative pedagogies that are flexible, committed, and, most importantly, rhetorical. The purpose of critical literacy is to see oneself and one's texts in context, as part of a vast network of possible selves and texts, each of which depends on shifting social relations and constant rewriting. Thus, to be an agent in this network is to be ever aware of the shifting, temporary situation of the text. And yet, importantly, it is necessary somehow to *write* oneself into the network, to momentarily identify as or with some discourse or some other text. This necessity, as Miller argues, makes itself manifest through a fictionalized stability, a temporary textuality that makes visible the moment of personal becoming public and political. Radical feminist manifestos and feminist heterotopias online offer us a clear view of that fictionalized stability, a stability dependent on text in order for it to work and to create responses, answers, other texts.

THE PROBLEM OF COMMUNITY

In her discussion of cultural studies approaches to composition, Reynolds encourages feminists in composition to investigate the possibilities of interruption in written texts, writing that compositionists must offer students better means of resistance to standard textual forms such as the rigidly structured, thesis-driven essay. Further, she writes, we need to rethink our own notions of "acceptable" texts and thus, perhaps, break down "some of the rigid boundaries that separate life and politics inside and outside the academy";[46] such negotiation of boundaries offers a tactical means of discursive agency.[47] Likewise, Caughie encourages compositionists to seize the discursive agency that comes between personal and political, authority and resistance. She writes that performative pedagogies self-consciously reproduce the structures of authority in order to undermine them; such pedagogies by necessity also authorize new subject positions.[48] But what are these new, liminal subject positions? I will argue that they are textually radical positions, dependent on personal consciousness as part of a temporarily stable, collective network.

While a key part of radical feminist textuality has been the move from personal consciousness to collective action, however, it is important to keep in mind the problematic status of women-only "safe space" in feminism, as well as the trenchant critiques of the idea of "community" in composition studies. Clearly, women-only space has served an important function in feminism, in that it offers an accepting, uncritical forum for discussion of women's issues. As hooks points out, however, such spaces have also served to silence dissensus in the interests of white hegemony:

In the early years of contemporary feminist movement, solidarity between women was often equated with the formation of "safe" spaces where groups of presumably like-minded women could come together, sharing ideas and experiences without fear of silencing or rigorous challenges. Groups sometimes disintegrated when the speaking of diverse opinions led to contestation, confrontation, and out-and-out conflict. It was common for individual dissenting voices to be silenced by the collective demand for harmony.[49]

Likewise, Audre Lorde writes, in a criticism of the white, middle-class heterosexual myopia that informs many discussions of feminism, that it "is a particular academic arrogance to assume any discussion of feminist theory without examining our many differences."[50] Lorde insists that we move beyond "mere tolerance" of difference and begin to see difference "as a fund of necessary polarities between which our creativity can spark like a dialectic."[51] It is crucial, then, that any definition of *collective* action be interpreted broadly enough to provide space for this dialectic.

Like women-only space, "community" in composition studies has functioned as a falsely optimistic idea that often elides difference. Like the concept of women-only space, too, "community" has been roundly critiqued, most notably by Joseph Harris. Harris notes, in *A Teaching Subject* and elsewhere, that the word "community" can soon become "empty and sentimental . . . [Community] tends to mean little more than a nicer, friendlier, fuzzier version of what came before."[52] Particularly troublesome, he writes, is the notion of an "academic discourse community," brought into prominence by such compositionists as David Bartholomae and Patricia Bizzell. Harris writes that the invocation of this term is a powerful rhetorical move, in that it offers us a way of examining student discourse without suggesting that they are slow or inept; "one can argue," he writes, "that the problem is less one of intelligence than socialization."[53] Further, the use of "community" makes visible our persuasive performance as teachers, the ways in which "we ask our students to acquire not only certain skills and data, but to try on new forms of thinking and talking about the world as well."[54] The problem with the concept's invocation, however, is that it elides the sociopolitical realm of language; just like separatist women's space, the concept of a discourse community sidesteps issues of discursive and material power relations.

Harris also offers the term "public" as a positive opposing term to "community," writing that what he finds most useful about the concept of *public* "is that it refers not to a group of people (like community) but to a kind of space and process, a point of contact that needs both to be created and continuously maintained."[55] Harris resists offering an ideal public sphere, since not all public debates offer anything close to universal access to all ideas and conflicts. Instead, he claims, public space is "a place where differences are made visible, and thus . . . the threat of conflict or even violence is always present. This means that we need to resist moves to romanticize conflict in order to argue for something more like *civility*, a willingness to live with difference."[56] Further, Harris writes:

> Thinking in terms of public rather than communal life can give us a way of describing the sort of talk that takes place *across* borders and constituencies. It suggests that we speak as public intellectuals when we talk with strangers rather than with the members of our own communities and disciplines (or of our own interdisciplinary cliques). And so what I do want to argue for here is a view of the classroom as a public space rather than as a kind of entry point into some imagined community of academic discourse.[57]

Like John Schilb's problematization of "collaboration" in *Between the Lines*[58] and Miller's reevaluation of "subjectivity" in *Rescuing the Subject*, Harris's discussion is part of a necessary *textualizing* of contexts and subjectivities that is a relatively recent phenomenon in the field of composition. This phenomenon points to an epistemology of social acts enacted and acted upon, not just in institutional and geographical contexts, but also in gendered, classed, raced, sexually oriented, "differenced" contexts.

In the space between private and public, personal consciousness and collective action, authority invoked and authority subverted, we may find Harris's "point of contact," a process of interaction and interruption that functions as the fictionalized stability necessary for writerly subjectivity. As Giroux and Shannon write, a performative pedagogy creates such a site, functioning as "a narrative space that affirms the contextual and the specific while simultaneously recognizing the ways in which such spaces are shot through with issues of power."[59] A performative pedagogy, that is, insists that we develop projects that reconstitute the traditional binary pairs of "margin/center, unity/difference, local/national, and public/private . . . through more complex representations of identification, belonging, and community."[60] The negotiation of identification, belonging, and community demands a literacy of networks, a rhetoric of collective identification. Networks and collectives are necessarily diverse, depending less on like-mindedness than discursive happenstance for their existence. While some networks do exist as part of a "community"—the example of the leftist underground network of the 1960s is instructive here—for the most part their existence is always already subject to negotiation. In the particular case of the 1960s' underground network, radical women subverted it in order to create a loose national collective of increasingly disparate groups. Likewise, feminists on the Internet have created spaces that themselves create a collective through anonymous or ambiguous participation. The points of contact in a network themselves constitute the network; it is through the process of using the network that one finds the temporary stability necessary for textual action.

NETWORK AND COLLECTIVE LITERACIES: THREE VIEWS

At the same time as feminist textuality online creates provocative and generative sites for social action, concerns about intellectual property and textual control threaten to hamper the network, just as similar concerns finished off the underground publishing network of the radical feminist movement in the late 1960s. As radical feminist manifestos began as a textual invocation of collaborative-yet-ambiguous identity for a collective and then morphed into a credited/copyrighted slip in an anthology, student-authored texts—particularly online texts—have become increasingly plagued by questions of textual ownership.[61] At what point does the public purposiveness of the manifesto become the dated relic of an outmoded argument? At what point, that is, does a text lose its flexibility and no longer signify collective, literate action? To answer these questions, and to point toward a radical feminist textual subjectivity, I offer three examples of network/collective literacy.

The first view is Cathy Fleischer's "Forming an Interactive Literacy in the Writing Classroom," in which we read about "Sarah," a student whose passion for writing and revision virtually disappeared by the time she was a sophomore in college. Fleischer describes the event in Bakhtinian terms, writing that Sarah's internally persuasive discourse was overcome, ultimately, by the authoritative discourse of academia. Sarah's struggle with authoritative discourse—a struggle between the "conforming literacy" of school and the "in-forming" literacy of community—provides the groundwork for Fleischer's argument for an "interactive literacy," one that takes place in writing classrooms conceived of as "literacy sites."[62] These sites, according to Fleischer, are "interactive places where students are encouraged to let their internally persuasive discourses, their own in-formed literacies, serve as the basis for their necessary interaction with academic talk and writing."[63] Fleischer writes:

> The task as I see it is not to continue to provide introduction after introduction to various authoritative discourses, but rather to create a space in our classrooms where students' internally persuasive discourses are first celebrated and then analyzed as a way into examining what of value might be gleaned from an in-forming literacy and applied to this strange new world of college writing.[64]

Fleischer then describes a course sequence in which students first investigate language use in communities with which they already (individually) familiar, then in communities with which they are familiar as a collective (in this case, the high school writing classroom). Finally, the students write an ethnography of a language community within the university. Fleischer's purpose in this sequence is to teach students to value their own "in-forming" literacies and to place them in the context of the university's "conforming" literacy, resulting in "a kind of marriage which we hope results in a more interactive literacy than Sarah was able to practice."[65]

Kathryn Thoms Flannery offers a similarly interactive view of literacy in her essay "In Praise of the Local and Transitory." In this essay, Flannery weaves together Foucault's theories of power and Shirley Brice Heath's work in order to problematize compositionists' deep-seated "need to see ourselves as liberators" in the writing classroom.[66] Flannery offers an alternative conception of teaching writing, but resists making "global, universalizing claims" about it; instead, she offers what she sees as a Foucaultian alternative, one that makes use of "subjugated, local knowledges."[67] Flannery describes a graduate-level introduction to literacy studies in which students were finally dismayed by Heath's *Ways with Words* because her project, so promising in its alternative view of literacy, met its demise soon after Heath left the communities in which she'd done her study.[68] Flannery's point, however, is that the importance of Heath's project lies in its status as "local, specific, and necessarily temporary. The aim should be not to institutionalize Heath's project but to support, wherever possible, the proliferation of other local, specific, and necessarily temporary projects."[69]

Flannery looks specifically to Foucault's critique of universalizing theories to further her point. She writes:

> if one understands how unitary theories work to cancel out the other, to silence the voices that do not fit, to erase the parts of the picture that detract from the balance of some idealized whole, then local and fragmentary knowledges that challenge the wholeness of global theories become of critical importance.[70]

Flannery argues for a valuing of multiple literacies and approaches to literacy education, but also cautions against viewing this argument as one for mere pluralism, especially if that pluralism means that teachers only allow diversity as long as it can be "centrally controlled or managed."[71] Instead, she writes that recognizing multiplicity means resisting the urge to "institutionalize the content, the specifics, or the pedagogies of literacy learning."[72] That is, she writes, we must make our local and specific knowledges available through an unknowable network of students, teachers, and communities, in order to "make knowledges available for their use, to be used for their own ends, so that new knowledges can be made in ways we do not fully understand and cannot control."[73]

Finally, in "Collaboration, Resistance, and the Teaching of Writing," Suzanne Clark and Lisa Ede note that advocates of collaborative learning in the composition classroom often do not take into account the cultural and ideological forces at work in the classroom, instead implying "that the classroom can function as a neutral site of learning, a magic epistemological circle of chalk dust separating students and teachers from the world at large."[74] Drawing from a psychoanalytic perspective, Clark and Ede argue for a valuation of "ignorance," which they describe as "the repressed other of knowledge we might call upon to serve as a place for resistance."[75] They write that a conception of resistance as ignorance may allow the teacher to give up his or her domination of knowledge-construction in the classroom; further, such a conception may allow students "finally speak what has resisted and has appeared as silence."[76] They write:

> however expert we are, we, as teachers, do not ever know what our students will learn from us, and yet that is precisely what our students think we know. The moment of learning is the moment of ignorance, of seeing the gap, the blank—feeling the lack. Our situation is paradoxically hopeful: not only should we not work to impose on our students what we think it means to be literate, but, no matter how hard we try, we cannot entirely do so. Repression does not exercise a totalitarian control over either the political or the personal unconscious.[77]

Clark and Ede insist that we focus on the rhetorical situation of the classroom itself, "because it reminds us that teachers must always contend with the authority that their position constructs; students must always deal with their own lack of authority."[78] Like Miller, Clark and Ede recognize the precarious position of a student writer "whispering in the Coliseum," for example, occupying a seemingly contradictory position of empowered writer and disempowered student.

It is perhaps no surprise that we have resisted the seemingly contradictory positions occupied by radical feminists and student writers alike, given that we are not always comfortable with ambiguity ourselves. Whether we see it as a struggle between "in-forming" and "conforming" literacies, "subjugated, local knowledges" and "global, universalizing claims," or knowledge and its repressed other, ignorance, we resist opening the site *between* as a place for textual action; rather, we wish to collapse that space or negate it, privilege the "resistant" site at the expense of the "dominant" one, all in the interests of an emancipatory textual action to come later. Radical feminist textuality, however, is a discourse of the moment; with its emphasis on both the personal *and* the political, the text *and* the network, it forms a particularly telling example of writerly subjectivity, mediating between the worlds of gender politics and print culture in order to change (and yet resist) both.

What would it mean to enact a performative pedagogy that valued a radical feminist subjectivity? First and foremost, it would mean engaging ourselves, making the personal political and *textual*, and thus creating a pedagogical site in which our students gain and create

knowledge that enriches them, us, and all of our collectives and networks. It would mean seeing feminist history as an ideological project,
constructed, for better or worse, according to the interests of those
writing the books. Thus, it might mean subverting standard histories
of feminism in composition, scarce as they may be, to account for the
singularity of radical feminist textuality as it appears in the late 1960s
and on the Internet. A performative pedagogy of radical feminist textuality would insist on valuing *different* voices and "ways of knowing"
for women, some of them nurturing and relational and some of them
openly confrontational and resistant to "nurturespeak." Finally, it
would emphasize that space *between*—between personal and political,
resistance and authority, private and public, text and network, writer
and reader—in which textual subjectivity is possible.

NOTES

INTRODUCTION

1. Robin Morgan, "Introduction," in *Sisterhood is Powerful: An Anthology of Writings from the Women's Liberation Movement,* ed. Robin Morgan (New York: Random, 1970), xv.

2. Lester Faigley, "Literacy After the Revolution," *College Composition and Communication* 48 (1997): 41.

3. Rosemarie Tong notes that while it is "simplistic" to equate women's rights groups with liberal reformism and women's liberation groups with radical feminism, she also writes that the equation "is not entirely inaccurate" (45). It is important to keep in mind, with Tong, that many feminists "fall between the cracks" of such divisions (46). (Rosemarie Tong, *Feminist Thought: A More Comprehensive Introduction,* 2nd ed. [Boulder: Westview Press, 1998]).

4. Susan Miller, "Writing Theory::Theory Writing," *Methods and Methodologies in Composition Research,* eds. Gesa E. Kirsch and Patricia A. Sullivan (Carbondale: Southern Illinois University Press, 1992), 83.

5. Lynn Worsham, guest lecture, University of South Florida, Tampa (24 January 1997).

1. FEMINISM, COMPOSITION, AND RE-HISTORY

1. Cheryl Glenn, *Rhetoric Retold: Regendering the Tradition from Antiquity Through the Renaissance* (Carbondale: Southern Illinois University Press, 1997); Jacqueline Jones Royster, *Traces in a Stream: Literacy and Social Change Among African-American Women* (Pittsburgh: University of Pittsburgh Press, 2000).

2. Suzanne Clark, "Argument and Composition," in *Feminism and Composition Studies: In Other Words,* eds. Susan C. Jarratt and Lynn Worsham (New York: MLA, 1998), 97.

3. Suzanne Clark, "Rhetoric, Social Construction, and Gender: Is It Bad to Be Sentimental?" in *Writing Theory and Critical Theory,* eds. John Clifford and John Schilb (New York: MLA, 1994), 96–108; JoAnn Campbell, ed., *Toward a Feminist Rhetoric: The Writing of Gertrude Buck* (Pittsburgh: University of Pittsburgh Press, 1996); Susan Miller, "The Feminization of Composition," in *The Politics of Writing Instruction: Postsecondary,* eds. Richard H. Bullock and John Trimbur (Portsmouth, NJ: Boynton/Cook-Heinemann, 1991), 39–53.

4. See in particular Worsham's "Writing against Writing: The Predicament of Ecriture Féminine in Composition Studies" in *Contending with Words: Composition and Rhetoric in a Postmodern Age,* eds. Patricia Harkin and John Schilb (New York: MLA, 1991): 82–104.

5. Nancy Hartsock, "Postmodernism and Political Change: Issues for Feminist Theory," in *Feminist Interpretations of Michel Foucault,* ed. Susan J. Hekman (University Park: The Pennsylvania State University Press, 1996), 43.

6. Sabina Lovibond, "Feminism and Postmodernism," in *Postmodernism: A Reader,* ed. Thomas Docherty (New York: Columbia University Press, 1993), 395.

7. Hartsock, 46.

8. Monique Deveaux, "Feminism and Empowerment: A Critical Reading of Foucault," in Hekman, 217.

9. Judith Goleman, *Working Theory: Critical Composition Studies for Students and Teachers* (Westport: Bergin & Garvey, 1995), 1.

10. Donald F. Bouchard, "Introduction," in *Language, Counter-Memory, Practice: Selected Essays and Interviews by Michel Foucault,* by Michel Foucault, ed. and intro. by Donald F. Bouchard (Ithaca: Cornell University Press, 1977), 22.

11. Michel Foucault, "Theatrum Philosophicum," in Foucault, *Language,* 175–76.

12. Michel Foucault, "Nietzsche, Genealogy, History," in Foucault, *Language,* 144.

13. The "Belenky collective" has become one of the usual ways to refer to this group of authors. For clarity's sake, however, I will refer to this group as

the "Belenky collaborative," since I use "collective" to refer to a specific type of second-wave feminist grouping.

14. Alice Echols, *Daring to Be Bad: Radical Feminism in America 1967–1975* (Minneapolis: University of Minnesota Press, 1989), 285.

15. Evelyn Ashton-Jones and Dene Kay Thomas, "Composition, Collaboration, and Women's Ways of Knowing: A Conversation with Mary Belenky," *Journal of Advanced Composition* 10 (1990), 275.

16. Eileen E. Schell, "The Costs of Caring: 'Feminism' and Contingent Women Workers in Composition Studies," in Jarratt and Worsham, 76.

17. Louise Wetherbee Phelps and Janet Emig, "Editors' Reflections: Vision and Interpretation," in *Feminine Principles and Women's Experience in American Composition and Rhetoric,* eds. Louise Wetherbee Phelps and Janet Emig (Pittsburgh: University of Pittsburgh Press, 1995), 408.

18. Schell, 76.

19. Foucault, "Nietzsche," 144.

20. Laura Brady, "The Reproduction of Othering," in Jarratt and Worsham, 25–26.

21. Ibid., 25.

22. Schell, 75.

23. Jennifer M. Gore, *The Struggle for Pedagogies: Critical and Feminist Discourses as Regimes of Truth* (New York: Routledge, 1993), 70.

24. Cynthia L. Caywood and Gillian R. Overing, eds. and intro., *Teaching Writing: Pedagogy, Gender, and Equity.* Albany: State University of New York Press, 1987), xii.

25. Ibid., xiv.

26. Cynthia L. Caywood and Gillian R. Overing, "Writing Across the Curriculum: a Model for a Workshop and a Call for Change," in Caywood and Overing, *Teaching,* 198.

27. Ibid., 22.

28. Rebecca Blevins Faery, "Women and Writing Across the Curriculum: Learning and Liberation," in Caywood and Overing, *Teaching,* 202.

29. Carol A. Stanger, "The Sexual Politics of the One-To-One Tutorial Approach and Collaborative Learning," in Caywood and Overing, *Teaching,* 40.

30. Elisabeth Däumer and Sandra Runzo, "Transforming the Composition Classroom," in Caywood and Overing, *Teaching*, 48–49.

31. Downplaying the necessary infantilization of students that accompanies such an approach, Däumer and Runzo write that to "transform the composition classroom into a feminist language classroom," we must:

> . . . draw on the life and practices of our first language teacher, the mother, for an understanding of the complexities of our role as teachers; and for the articulation of guiding values and ideals which stem from a radical critique of institutionalized mothering and the resultant vision of mothering as a primary locus for the transmission and the creation of women's language and culture. (49)

32. Elizabeth A. Flynn, "Composing as a Woman," *College Composition and Communication* 39 (1988): 423.

33. Ibid., 425.

34. Ibid.

35. Clark, "Argument," 97.

36. Flynn, "Composing," 425.

37. Pamela Annas, "Silences: Feminist Language Research and the Teaching of Writing," in Caywood and Overing, *Teaching*, 3.

38. Joy Ritchie, "Confronting the 'Essential' Problem: Reconnecting Feminist Theory and Pedagogy," *Journal of Advanced Composition* 10 (1990): 269.

39. Harriet Malinowitz, "A Feminist Critique of Writing in the Disciplines," in Jarratt and Worsham, 305.

40. Ibid.

41. Rosalyn Fraad Baxandall, "Catching the Fire," in *The Feminist Memoir Project: Voices from Women's Liberation*, eds. Rachel Blau DuPlessis and Ann Snitow (New York: Three Rivers Press, 1998), 214.

42. Susan C. Jarratt, "Introduction: As We Were Saying . . . ," in Jarratt and Worsham, 4.

43. Ibid., 9.

44. Lynn Worsham, "After Words: A Choice of Words Remains," in Jarratt and Worsham, 352.

45. Don Kraemer, "No Exit: A Play of Literacy and Gender," *Journal of Advanced Composition* 10: 313.

46. Susan C. Jarratt, "Feminism and Composition: The Case for Conflict," in Harkin and Schilb, 106.

47. Ibid., 106, 121.

48. Worsham, "Writing," 95.

49. Phelps and Emig, "Editors'," 409.

50. Evelyn Ashton-Jones, "Collaboration, Conversation, and the Politics of Gender," in Phelps and Emig, *Feminine*, 10.

51. Ibid.

52. Joy Ritchie and Kate Ronald, "Riding Long Coattails, Subverting Tradition: The Tricky Business of Feminists Teaching Rhetoric(s)," in Jarratt and Worsham, 231.

53. Ibid.

54. Ibid., 234–35.

55. Elizabeth Flynn, "Composition Studies from a Feminist Perspective," in Bullock and Trimbur, 47.

56. Schell, 74.

57. Foucault, "Theatrum," 175–76.

58. Schell, 74–75.

59. Ibid., 80.

60. Louise Wetherbee Phelps, "Becoming a Warrior: Lessons of the Feminist Workplace," in Phelps and Emig, 289.

61. Rachel Blau DuPlessis and Ann Snitow, "A Feminist Memoir Project," in DuPlessis and Snitow, 8.

2. REWRITING RADICAL WOMEN

1. Solanas, who had appeared in Andy Warhol's films *I, a Man* and *Bikeboy* in 1967, shot and near-fatally wounded Warhol in 1968 after claiming that he had conspired with publisher Maurice Girodias to appropriate her work. The shooting and the events leading up to it are portrayed in the 1996 film starring Lili Taylor.

2. Robin Morgan, *Going Too Far: The Personal Chronicle of a Feminist* (New York: Random House, 1977), 119.

3. See, for example, Sara Evans's *Personal Politics: The Roots of Women's Liberation in the Civil Rights Movement and the New Left* (New York: Vintage, 1979).

4. Echols, 139.

5. Beverly Jones and Judith Brown, "Toward a Female Liberation Movement," in *Voices from Women's Liberation,* ed. Leslie B. Tanner (New York: Signet, 1971), 366.

6. Ibid., 413.

7. Morgan, *Going,* 157

8. Bonnie Kreps, "Radical Feminism I," in *Radical Feminism,* eds. Anne Koedt, Ellen Levine, and Anita Rapone (New York: Quadrangle, 1973), 239.

9. Echols, 52.

10. Jo Freeman, *The Politics of Women's Liberation: A Case Study of an Emerging Social Movement and Its Relation to the Policy Process* (New York: David McKay, 1975), 51.

11. Ibid.

12. New York Radical Feminists, "Politics of the Ego: A Manifesto for N.Y. Radical Feminists," in Koedt, Levine, and Rapone, 379.

13. Redstockings, "Redstockings Manifesto," in *Feminism in Our Time: The Essential Writings, World War II to the Present,* ed. Miriam Schneir (New York: Vintage-Random House, 1994), 127.

14. Morgan, *Going,* 156.

15. Barbara Susan, "About My Consciousness-Raising," in Tanner, 243.

16. Ibid.

17. Mary Ann Weathers, "An Argument for Black Women's Revolution As a Revolutionary Force," in Tanner, 303.

18. Ibid., 304.

19. Ibid., 306.

20. Redstockings, 108.

21. The Radicalesbians (formerly the "Lavender Menace," so titled in response to Betty Friedan's remarks on lesbianism) were a lesbian feminist collective that protested homophobia in the women's movement at the Second Congress to Unite Women (1970). Their own position paper, "The Woman-

Identified Woman," began a successful struggle to make lesbian rights part of the second-wave feminists' agenda (Schneir 160–61). See also the following note 33.

22. Juliet Mitchell, "Women: The Longest Revolution," in Schneir, 203.

23. Kreps, 235.

24. Ibid.

25. Redstockings, 128.

26. Eleanor Holmes Norton, "For Sadie and Maude," in Morgan, *Sisterhood*, 398–99.

27. Coletta Reid and Charlotte Bunch, "Revolution Begins at Home," in *Class & Feminism: A Collection of Essays from the Furies*, eds. Charlotte Bunch and Nancy Myron (Baltimore: Diana, 1974), 81.

28. Ibid., 72.

29. Rita Mae Brown, *A Plain Brown Rapper* (Oakland: Diana, 1976), 72–73.

30. Ibid., 55.

31. See Brown; see also Toni Cade's *The Black Woman: An Anthology* (New York: Signet, 1970), for example.

32. Echols, 10.

33. It was widely reported that Friedan had remarked that lesbian feminists were a "lavender menace" that would hurt the women's movement. The remark led to the eruption of the lesbian feminist movement, beginning with the twenty-member "Lavender Menace" that disrupted the Second Congress to Unite Women in 1970 (Schneir, 160).

34. bell hooks, *Teaching to Transgress: Education as the Practice of Freedom* (New York: Routledge, 1994), 49.

35. Ibid.

36. Carol Mattingly, "Valuing the Personal: Feminist Concerns for the Writing Classroom," in *Gender and Academe: Feminist Pedagogy and Politics*, eds. Sara Munson Deats and Lagretta Tallent Lenker (Lanham: Rowman & Littlefield, 1994), 153–54.

37. Ibid., 154.

38. Susan, 242.

39. Freeman, 86.

40. Ibid.

41. Echols, 116.

42. Morgan, *Going,* 72.

43. Redstockings, 128.

44. "Consciousness-Raising," in Tanner, 253.

45. Susan, 242.

46. Ibid.

47. Echols, 141

48. Ibid.

49. Ibid., 88.

50. Ibid., 88–89.

51. Redstockings, 129.

52. Joan Cassell, *A Group Called Women: Sisterhood & Symbolism in the Feminist Movement* (New York: David McKay, 1979), 149.

53. Ibid., 137.

54. Ibid., 140.

55. Joreen, "The Tyranny of Structurelessness," in Koedt, Levine, and Rapone, 285.

56. Cassell, 55.

57. Ibid.

58. Kathie Sarachild, "Feminist Consciousness Raising and 'Organizing': Outline Prepared for a Lake Villa Workshop, November, 1968," in Tanner, 154–55.

59. Ibid., 156.

60. Ibid., 157.

61. "Consciousness-Raising" 253–54.

62. Rosalyn Fraad Baxandall, "Catching the Fire," in DuPlessis and Snitow, 211.

63. Maren Lockwood Carden, *The New Feminist Movement* (New York: Russell Sage Foundation, 1974), 178.

64. Judith Hole and Ellen Levine, *Rebirth of Feminism* (New York: Quadrangle, 1971), 272.

65. Freeman, 112.

66. Echols, 93–94.

67. Qtd. in Hole and Levine, 269.

68. Freeman, 112.

69. Ibid.

70. Ibid.

71. Morgan, *Going*, 116.

72. Ibid.

73. Hole and Levine, 273.

74. Ibid., 274.

75. Carden, 65.

76. Hole and Levine, 271.

77. Freeman, 109–10.

78. Ibid., 110.

79. Ibid., 116.

80. Ibid.

81. Koedt, Levine, and Rapone, 365.

82. Morgan, *Going*, 119.

83. Ibid.

84. Black Women's Liberation Group, "Statement on Birth Control," in Morgan, *Sisterhood*, 406.

85. Redstockings, 127.

86. Ibid., 128.

87. Ibid.

88. New York Radical Feminists, 379.

89. Ibid.

90. Ibid., 382.

91. Ibid., 383

92. Shulamith Firestone, *The Dialectic of Sex: The Case for Feminist Revolution* (New York: Bantam, 1972), 10–11.

93. Kate Millett, *Sexual Politics* (New York: Avon, 1971).

94. Kate Millett, "Sexual Politics: A Manifesto for Revolution," in Koedt, Levine, and Rapone, 365.

95. Ibid., 366–67.

96. Southern Female Rights Union, "Southern Female Rights Union Program for Female Liberation," in Tanner, 114.

97. Ibid., 113.

98. Echols, 159.

99. Qtd. in Freddie Baer's "About Valerie Solanas," in *The SCUM Manifesto* by Valerie Solanas (1967; Rpt. San Francisco: AK, 1996), 58.

100. Dana Densmore, "A Year of Living Dangerously: 1968," in DuPlessis and Snitow, 75.

101. Shulamith Firestone, *Airless Spaces* (New York: Semiotext(e), 1998), 130.

102. Echols, 105.

103. Densmore, 78.

104. Solanas, 1.

105. Ibid., 45–46.

106. Freeman, 103.

107. Hole and Levine, 270.

108. Echols, 198.

109. Ibid, 201.

110. "Editorial: Notes from the Third Year," in Koedt, Levine, and Rapone, 300.

111. Carden, 98.

112. Freeman, 110.

113. Morgan, *Sisterhood*, 117.

114. Echols, 201.

3. FROM MANIFESTO TO MODEM

1. "Forward," *Wench*, 1996 <http://www.wench.com/> (12 September 1998).

2. Mimi Nguyen, "Original Statement." *Exoticize My Fist!* September 1997 <http://members.aol.com/ Critchicks/original.html> (20 June 2003).

3. "Perfect Woman Rant." *GiRLRiGHtS!* <http://www.mmotion.com/ grrrl/rants/perfect_ woman.html> (18 September 1998).

4. Mimi Nguyen, *Exoticize My Fist!* <http://members.aol.com/ Critchicks/index2.html> (20 June 2003).

5. Jay David Bolter, *Writing Space: The Computer, Hypertext, and the Remediation of Print*, 2nd ed. (Hillsdale: Lawrence Erlbaum, 2001), 38.

6. Ibid., 36.

7. Stuart Moulthrop and Nancy Kaplan, "They Became What They Beheld: The Futility of Resistance in the Space of Electronic Writing," in *Literacy and Computers: The Complications of Teaching and Learning with Technology*, eds. Cynthia L. Selfe and Susan Hilligoss (New York: MLA, 1994), 236.

8. Michael Joyce, "Siren Shapes: Exploratory and Constructive Hypertexts," *Academic Computing* Nov 1988, 11.

9. Johndan Johnson-Eilola, "Reading and Writing in Hypertext: Vertigo and Euphoria," in Selfe and Hilligoss, 201.

10. George Landow and Paul Delany, "Hypertext, Hypermedia, and Literary Studies: The State of the Art," in *Hypermedia and Literary Studies*, eds. Paul Delany and George Landow (Cambridge: MIT Press, 1990), 6.

11. Johndan Johnson-Eilola, *Nostalgic Angels: Rearticulating Hypertext Writing* (Norwood: Ablex, 1997).

12. Johnson-Eilola, "Reading," 196.

13. Michael Dertouzos, *What Will Be: How the New World of Information Will Change Our Lives* (New York: HarperEdge-HarperCollins, 1997), 42–43.

14. See Thompson; Cooper and Selfe.

15. Johnson-Eilola, "Reading," 196

16. See Coyle; Kendall.

17. Gail E. Hawisher and Cynthia L. Selfe, "Inventing Postmodern Identities: Hybrid and Transgressive Literacy Practices on the Web," in *Global Literacies and the World-Wide Web,* eds. Gail E. Hawisher and Cynthia L. Selfe (London: Routledge, 2000), 281.

18. Ibid., 284.

19. Mary J. Flores, "Computer Conferencing: Composing a Feminist Community of Writers," in *Computers and Community: Teaching Composition in the Twenty-First Century,* ed. Carolyn Handa (Portsmouth: Boynton/ Cook-Heinemann, 1990), 115.

20. Ibid., 108

21. Billie J. Wahlstrom, "Communication and Technology: Defining a Feminist Presence In Research and Practice," in Selfe and Hilligoss, 171.

22. Ibid., 181.

23. Ibid., 184.

24. See also Hawisher and Selfe, "Reflections on Computers and Composition Studies at the Century's End" in *Page to Screen: Taking Literacy into the Electronic Era,* ed. Ilana Snyder (New York: Routledge, 1998), 3–19.

25. Cynthia L. Selfe, "Technology in the English Classroom: Computers through the Lens of Feminist Theory," in Handa, 121.

26. Ibid., 132.

27. Ibid., 122.

28. Ibid., 123.

29. Ibid., 131.

30. Gail E. Hawisher and Patricia Sullivan "Women on the Networks: Searching for E-Spaces of Their Own," in Jarratt and Worsham, 173.

31. Ibid.

32. Ibid., 175.

33. Ibid., 178.

34. Ibid., 181.

35. Ibid., 179–80.

36. Ibid., 186.

37. SWLAB Moderators, "The soc.women.lesbian-and-bi Moderation Policy." 14 November 2000 <http://www.panix.com/~swlab-m/modpolicy. html> (25 June 2003), 7.4.

38. Ibid., 9.1–2, 9.4.

39. Stephanie Brail, "The Price of Admission: Harassment and Free Speech in the Wild, Wild West," in *Wired Women: Gender and New Realities in Cyberspace,* eds. Lynn Cherny and Elizabeth Reba Weise (Seattle: Seal Press, 1996), 147.

40. L. Jean Camp "We Are Geeks, and We Are Not Guys: The Systers Mailing List," in Cherny and Weise, 115.

41. Ibid.

42. Ibid.

43. Ibid., 120.

44. Ibid., 121.

45. Brail, 156–57.

46. Hawisher and Sullivan, 193.

47. Selfe, "Technology," 124–25.

48. Karen Coyle, "How Hard Can It Be?" in Cherny and Weise, 42.

49. Ibid., 45.

50. See Donna LeCourt and Luann Barnes, "Writing Multiplicity: Hypertext and Feminist Textual Politics," *Computers and Composition* 16 (1999): 55–71.

51. Nicholas C. Burbules, "Rhetorics of the Web: Hyperreading and Critical Literacy," in Snyder, 103.

52. Ibid., 104.

53. Freeman, 103.

54. "Forward," par. 7.

55. Ibid.

56. "About Wench," 1996 <http://www.wench.com/about/> (12 March 2002), par. 1, 3.

57. "Statement of Purpose," in *Feminista!* 3.1, 1998 <http://www.feminista.com/v3n1/from-the-editor.html# purpose> (20 June 2003).

58. "Client Services," in *Cybergrrl,* 2001 <http://www.cgim.com/service.html> (20 June 2003), par. 1–2.

59. "Online Entertainment," in *Cybergrrl,* 2000 <http://www.cgim.com/entertain.html> (13 March 2002), par. 1.

60. "About Femina," 2001 <http://femina.cybergrrl.com/about.html> (20 June 2003), par. 1.

61. Ibid., par. 3.

62. Nguyen, "Original," par. 1.

63. Nguyen, *Exoticize,* par. 16.

64. Nguyen, "Original," par. 1.

65. Ibid.

66. Susana L. Gallardo, "huh," in *Making Face, Making Soul: A Chicana Feminist Homepage* <http://chicanas.com/huh.html> (20 June 2003), par. 1–2; emphasis in original.

67. Susana L. Gallardo, "Chicanas Chingonas," in *Making Face, Making Soul: A Chicana Feminist Homepage,* 25 May 2001 <http://chicanas.com/chingonas.html> (20 June 2003), par. 1.

68. Canadian Women Internet Association (CWIA), 29 September 1999 <http://www.herplace.org/> (20 June 2003), par. 2.

69. Sheila Eastman, online posting 10 May 1999, in *CWIA Guestbook* <http://www.women.ca/cgi-bin/signguest.pl?guestfile=women.main&guesttitle=CWIA+Guestbook&mailto=femail@women.ca&mailsubj=CWIA+Guestbook> (14 May 1999), par. 1.

70. *The 3rd WWWave: Feminism for a New Millennium* <http://www.io.com/~wwwave/> (20 June 2003), par. 1.

71. Ibid., par. 3.

72. Ibid., par. 4–8.

73. Ibid., par. 12.

4. TEXTUALITY, PERFORMATIVITY, AND NETWORK LITERACIES

1. Nguyen, "Original," par. 1.

2. hooks, *Teaching*, 19.

3. Carmen Luke, "Feminist Politics in Radical Pedagogy," in *Feminisms and Critical Pedagogy*, eds. Carmen Luke and Jennifer Gore (New York: Routledge, 1992), 38.

4. Ibid., 25.

5. As Pamela J. Caughie notes, the term "performativity" comes initially from the work of J. L. Austin (but has been elaborated by Derrida and Judith Butler, most notably), who distinguishes between constative and performative statements; the performative "is not *about* something but *does* something. It does not refer to some set of circumstances existing prior to or apart from it; rather, it *produces* what it is supposedly about, brings some set of circumstances into existence." (Pamela J. Caughie, "Passing as Pedagogy: Feminism in[to] Cultural Studies," in *English Studies/Culture Studies*, eds. Isaiah Smithson and Nancy Ruff [Urbana: University of Illinois Press, 1994], 93).

6. Perhaps the most topical use of Foucault's metaphor is in Jeffrey R. Galin and Joan Latchaw's "Defining Heterotopias," in *Kairos* 3.1 <http://english.ttu.edu/kairos/ 3.1/coverweb/galin/index.htm> (Spring 1998). Drawing from Foucault, Galin and Latchaw define heterotopias as lived spaces such as cemeteries, formal gardens, and libraries (for Galin and Latchaw, *online* libraries and archives), which have a precise, determined function within the culture. Heterotopias are linked "to slices in time," particularly in the case of library-as-archive and cemeteries; they "presuppose a system of opening and closing that both isolates them and makes them penetrable"; they often require a rite of passage, and even the ones that seem publicly accessible hide certain exclusions.

7. Susan Miller, *Rescuing the Subject: A Critical Introduction to Rhetoric and the Writer* (Carbondale: Southern Illinois University Press, 1989), 11.

8. Ibid., 149.

9. Ibid., 3.

10. Ibid., 35.

11. Ibid., 149.

12. Ibid., 160.

13. Ibid., 162–63.

14. Ibid., 164.

15. Ibid., 170.

16. hooks, *Teaching*, 13.

17. Ibid., 15.

18. Ibid., 21.

19. Henry A. Giroux and Patrick Shannon, "Cultural Studies and Pedagogy as Performative Practice: Toward an Introduction," in *Education and Cultural Studies: Toward a Performative Practice*, eds. Henry A. Giroux and Patrick Shannon (New York: Routledge, 1997), 2.

20. Ibid., 3.

21. Ibid., 7.

22. Ibid., 6.

23. Ibid., 8.

24. hooks, *Teaching*, 194.

25. Ibid., 202.

26. Giroux and Shannon, 8.

27. Luke, 49.

28. Kreps, 235.

29. bell hooks, *Outlaw Culture: Resisting Representations* (New York: Routledge, 1994), 3.

30. James Berlin, "Composition Studies and Cultural Studies: Collapsing Boundaries," in *Into the Field: The Site of Composition Studies*, ed. Anne Ruggles Gere (New York: MLA, 1993), 100.

31. Ibid., 109.

32. Ibid.

33. Ibid., 112.

34. Diana George and Diana Shoos, "Issues of Subjectivity and Resistance: Cultural Studies in the Composition Classroom," in *Cultural Studies in the English Classroom*, eds. James Berlin and Michael J. Vivion (Portsmouth: Boynton/Cook-Heinemann, 1992), 200.

35. Ibid., 209.

36. Caughie, 90.

37. Ibid.

38. Ibid., 78.

39. Ibid., 83.

40. Ibid., 92.

41. Nedra Reynolds, "Interrupting Our Way to Agency: Feminist Cultural Studies and Composition," in Jarratt and Worsham, 60.

42. Ibid., 66.

43. Ibid., 59.

44. Lisa R. Langstraat, "'Hypermasculinity' in Cultural Studies and Composition: Mapping a Feminist Response," *Composition Forum* 7 (1996): 1–2.

45. Ibid., 6–7.

46. Reynolds, 71.

47. Ibid., 72.

48. Caughie, 92.

49. hooks, *Outlaw*, 65.

50. Audre Lorde, "The Master's Tools Will Never Dismantle the Master's House," in *Sister Outsider: Essays and Speeches by Audre Lorde* (Freedom: Crossing, 1984), 110.

51. Ibid., 111.

52. Joseph Harris, *A Teaching Subject: Composition Since 1966* (Upper Saddle River: Prentice Hall, 1997), 99.

53. Ibid., 102.

54. Ibid.

55. Ibid., 108–09.

56. Ibid., 109.

57. Ibid.

58. John Schilb, *Between the Lines: Relating Composition Theory and Literary Theory* (Portsmouth: Boynton/Cook-Heinemann, 1996).

59. Giroux and Shannon, 4.

60. Ibid., 8.

61. See Andrea Lunsford et al., "What Matters Who Writes? What Matters Who Responds? Issues of Ownership in the Writing Classroom," *Kairos* 1.1 (1996) <http://english.ttu.edu/kairos/1.1/ features/lunsford/title.html> (25 June 2003).

62. Cathy Fleischer, "Forming an Interactive Literacy in the Writing Classroom," in Berlin and Vivion, 182–99. Fleischer writes:

> What Bakhtin calls authoritative discourse could be named as well as a *conforming literacy*, a literacy defined by the school rules and regulations, measured by students' adherence to certain forms and genres. Such a literacy might be seen in contrast to an *in-forming* literacy, the literacy students bring to school settings, whose forms arise from the internally persuasive discourses of their own language backgrounds. (184)

63. Ibid., 186.

64. Ibid.

65. Ibid., 198.

66. Kathryn Thoms Flannery, "In Praise of the Local and Transitory," in *The Right to Literacy,* eds. Andrea A. Lunsford, Helene Moglen, and James Slevin (New York: MLA, 1990), 208.

67. Ibid.

68. Shirley Brice Heath, *Ways with Words: Language, Life, and Work in Communities and Classrooms* (London: Cambridge University Press, 1983).

69. Flannery, 210.

70. Ibid., 210–11.

71. Ibid., 213.

72. Ibid.

73. Ibid.

74. Suzanne Clark and Lisa Ede, "Collaboration, Resistance, and the Teaching of Writing," in Lunsford, Moglen, and Slevin, 278.

75. Ibid., 282. See also Sharon Todd's "Psychoanalytic Questions, Pedagogical Possibilities, and Authority: Encountering the 'And'" (In Giroux and Shannon, 67–78).

76. Ibid.

77. Ibid., 282–83.

78. Ibid., 281.

WORKS CITED

"About Femina." 2001 [cited 20 June 2003]. Available from World Wide Web: <http://femina.cybergrrl.com/about.html>.

"About Wench." *Wench*. 1996 [cited 12 March 2002]. Available from World Wide Web: <http://www.wench.com/about/>.

Annas, Pamela. "Silences: Feminist Language Research and the Teaching of Writing." In Caywood and Overing, 3–17.

Ashton-Jones, Evelyn. "Collaboration, Conversation, and the Politics of Gender." In Phelps and Emig, 5–26.

Ashton-Jones, Evelyn, and Dene Kay Thomas. "Composition, Collaboration, and Women's Ways of Knowing: A Conversation with Mary Belenky." *Journal of Advanced Composition* 10 (1990): 275–92.

Baer, Freddie. "About Valerie Solanas." In Solanas, 51–60.

Baxandall, Rosalyn Fraad. "Catching the Fire." In DuPlessis and Snitow, 208–24.

Beauvoir, Simone de. *The Second Sex*. Trans. H.M. Parshley. New York: Vintage, 1989.

Berlin, James, and Michael J. Vivion, eds. *Cultural Studies in the English Classroom*. Portsmouth: Boynton/Cook-Heinemann, 1992.

Berlin, James. "Composition Studies and Cultural Studies: Collapsing Boundaries." In *Into the Field: The Site of Composition Studies,* ed. Anne Ruggles Gere, 99–116. New York: MLA, 1993.

Bishop, Wendy. "Learning Our Own Ways to Situate Composition and Feminist Studies in the English Department." *Journal of Advanced Composition* 10 (1990): 339–55.

Black Women's Liberation Group. "Statement on Birth Control." In Morgan, *Sisterhood*, 404–06.

Bolter, Jay David. *Writing Space: The Computer, Hypertext, and the Remediation of Print*. 2nd ed. Hillsdale: Lawrence Erlbaum, 2001.

Brady, Laura. "The Reproduction of Othering." In Jarratt and Worsham, 21–44.

Brail, Stephanie. "The Price of Admission: Harassment and Free Speech in the Wild, Wild West." In Cherny and Weise, 141–57.

Brodkey, Linda. "On the Subjects of Class and Gender in 'The Literacy Letters'" *College English* 51 (1989): 125–41.

Brown, Rita Mae. *A Plain Brown Rapper*. Oakland: Diana Press, 1976.

Bullock, Richard H., and John Trimbur, eds. *The Politics of Writing Instruction: Postsecondary*. Portsmouth: Boynton/Cook-Heinemann, 1991.

Bunch, Charlotte, and Nancy Myron, eds. *Class & Feminism: A Collection of Essays from the Furies*. Baltimore: Diana, 1974.

Burbules, Nicholas C. "Rhetorics of the Web: Hyperreading and Critical Literacy." In *Page to Screen: Taking Literacy into the Electronic Era*, ed. Ilana Snyder, 102–22. New York: Routledge, 1998.

Camp, L. Jean. "We Are Geeks, and We Are Not Guys: The Systers Mailing List." In Cherny and Weise, 114–25.

Campbell, JoAnn, ed. *Toward a Feminist Rhetoric: The Writing of Gertrude Buck*. Pittsburgh: University of Pittsburgh Press, 1996.

"Canadian Women's Internet Association." 29 September 1999 [cited 20 June 2003]. Available from World Wide Web: <http://www.herplace.org/>.

Carden, Maren Lockwood. *The New Feminist Movement*. New York: Russell Sage Foundation, 1974.

Cassell, Joan. *A Group Called Women: Sisterhood & Symbolism in the Feminist Movement*. New York: David McKay, 1979.

Caughie, Pamela L. "Passing as Pedagogy: Feminism in(to) Cultural Studies." In Smithson and Ruff, 76–93.

Caywood, Cynthia L., and Gillian R. Overing. "Writing Across the Curriculum: A Model for a Workshop and a Call for Change." In Caywood and Overing, *Feminism*, 185–200.

————, eds. and intro. *Teaching Writing: Pedagogy, Gender, and Equity.* Albany: State University of New York Press, 1987.

Cherny, Lynn, and Elizabeth Reba Weise, eds. *Wired Women: Gender and New Realities in Cyberspace.* Seattle: Seal Press, 1996.

Clark, Suzanne. "Argument and Composition." In Jarratt and Worsham, 94–99.

————. "Rhetoric, Social Construction, and Gender: Is It Bad to Be Sentimental?" In Clifford and Schilb, 96–108.

Clark, Suzanne, and Lisa Ede. "Collaboration, Resistance, and the Teaching of Writing." In Lunsford, Moglen, and Slevin, 276–85.

"Client Services." *Cybergrrl, Inc.* 2001 [cited 20 June 2003]. Available from World Wide Web: <http://www.cgim.com/service.html>.

Clifford, John, and John Schilb, eds. *Writing Theory and Critical Theory.* New York: MLA, 1994.

"Consciousness Raising." In Tanner, 253–54.

Cooper, Marilyn M., and Cynthia L. Selfe. "Computer Conferences and Learning: Authority, Resistance, and Internally Persuasive Discourse." *College English* 52 (1990): 847–69.

Coyle, Karen. "How Hard Can It Be?" In Cherny and Weise, 42–55.

Däumer, Elisabeth, and Sandra Runzo. "Transforming the Composition Classroom." In Caywood and Overing, 45–62.

Densmore, Dana. "A Year of Living Dangerously: 1968." In DuPlessis and Snitow, 71–89.

Dertouzos, Michael. *What Will Be: How the New World of Information Will Change Our Lives.* New York: HarperEdge-HarperCollins, 1997.

Deveaux, Monique. "Feminism and Empowerment: A Critical Reading of Foucault." In Hekman, 211–38.

DuPlessis, Rachel Blau, and Ann Snitow. "A Feminist Memoir Project." In DuPlessis and Snitow, 3–24.

————, eds. *The Feminist Memoir Project: Voices from Women's Liberation.* New York: Three Rivers Press, 1998.

Eastman, Sheila. Online posting. *CWIA Guestbook.* 10 May 1999 [cited 14 May 1999]. Available from World Wide Web: <http://www.women.ca/cgi-bin/signguest.pl?guestfile=women.main&guesttitle=CWIA+Guestbook&mailto=femail@women.ca&mailsubj=CWIA+Guestbook>.

Echols, Alice. *Daring to Be Bad: Radical Feminism in America 1967–1975*. Minneapolis: University of Minnesota Press, 1989.

Evans, Sara. *Personal Politics: The Roots of Women's Liberation in the Civil Rights Movement and the New Left*. New York: Vintage, 1979.

"Editorial: Notes from the Third Year." In Koedt, Levine, and Rapone, 300–01.

Faery, Rebecca Blevins. "Women and Writing Across the Curriculum: Learning and Liberation." In Caywood and Overing, 201–12.

Faigley, Lester. "Literacy After the Revolution." *College Composition and Communication* 48 (1997): 30–43.

Firestone, Shulamith. *Airless Spaces*. New York: Semiotext(e), 1998.

——— . *The Dialectic of Sex: The Case for Feminist Revolution*. New York: Bantam, 1972.

Flannery, Kathryn Thoms. "In Praise of the Local and Transitory." In Lunsford, Moglen, and Slevin, 208–14.

Fleischer, Cathy. "Forming an Interactive Literacy in the Writing Classroom." In Berlin and Vivion, 182–99.

Flores, Mary J. "Computer Conferencing: Composing a Feminist Community of Writers." In Handa, 106–17.

Flynn, Elizabeth A. "Composing as a Woman." *College Composition and Communication* 39 (1988): 423–35.

——— . "Composition Studies from a Feminist Perspective." In Bullock and Trimbur, 137–54.

"Forward." *Wench*. 1996 [cited 12 November 1998]. Available from World Wide Web: <http://www.wench.com/>.

Foucault, Michel. *Language, Counter-Memory, Practice: Selected Essays and Interviews by Michel Foucault*. Ed. and intro. by Donald F. Bouchard. Ithaca: Cornell University Press, 1977.

——— . "Theatrum Philosophicum." In Foucault, *Language*, 165–96.

——— . "Nietzsche, Genealogy, History." In Foucault, *Language*, 139–64.

Freeman, Jo. *The Politics of Women's Liberation: A Case Study of an Emerging Social Movement and Its Relation to the Policy Process*. New York: David McKay, 1975.

Galin, Jeffrey R., and Joan Latchaw. "Defining Heterotopias." *Kairos* 3.1 (Spring 1998) [cited 25 May 2003]. Available from World Wide Web: <http://english. ttu.edu/kairos/3.1/coverweb/galin/heterotopiadef.htm>.

Gallardo, Susana L. "Chicanas Chingonas." *Making Face, Making Soul: A Chicana Feminist Homepage* [online]. 25 May 2001 [cited 20 June 2003]. Available from World Wide Web: <http://chicanas.com/chingonas.html>.

———. "huh." *Making Face, Making Soul: A Chicana Feminist Homepage.* [Cited 20 June 2003]. Available from World Wide Web: <http://chicanas.com/huh.html>.

George, Diana, and Diana Shoos. "Issues of Subjectivity and Resistance: Cultural Studies in the Composition Classroom." In Berlin and Vivion, 200–10.

Giroux, Henry A., and Patrick Shannon. "Cultural Studies and Pedagogy as Performative Practice: Toward an Introduction." In Giroux and Shannon, 1–9.

———, eds. *Education and Cultural Studies: Toward a Performative Practice.* Eds. Henry A. Giroux and Patrick Shannon. New York: Routledge, 1997.

Glenn, Cheryl. *Rhetoric Retold: Regendering the Tradition from Antiquity Through the Renaissance.* Carbondale: Southern Illinois University Press, 1997.

Goleman, Judith. *Working Theory: Critical Composition Studies for Students and Teachers.* Westport: Bergin & Garvey, 1995.

Gore, Jennifer M. *The Struggle for Pedagogies: Critical and Feminist Discourses as Regimes of Truth.* New York: Routledge, 1993.

Goulston, Wendy. "Women Writing." In Caywood and Overing, 19–30.

Handa, Carolyn, ed. *Computers and Community: Teaching Composition in the Twenty-First Century.* Portsmouth: Boynton/Cook-Heinemann, 1990.

Harkin, Patricia, and John Schilb, eds. *Contending with Words: Composition and Rhetoric in a Postmodern Age.* New York: MLA, 1991.

Harris, Joseph. *A Teaching Subject: Composition Since 1966.* Upper Saddle River: Prentice Hall, 1997.

Hartsock, Nancy C. M. "Postmodernism and Political Change: Issues for Feminist Theory." In Hekman, 39–55.

Hawisher, Gail E., and Cynthia L. Selfe. "Inventing Postmodern Identities: Hybrid and Transgressive Literacy Practices on the Web." In *Global*

Literacies and the World-Wide Web, eds. Gail E. Hawisher and Cynthia L. Selfe. London: Routledge, 2000. 277–89.

———. "Reflections on Computers and Composition Studies at the Century's End." In *Page to Screen: Taking Literacy into the Electronic Era,* ed. Ilana Snyder, 3–19. New York: Routledge, 1998.

Hawisher, Gail E., and Patricia Sullivan. "Women on the Networks: Searching for E-Spaces of Their Own." In Jarratt and Worsham, 172–97.

Hays, Janice. "Intellectual Parenting and a Developmental Feminist Pedagogy of Writing." In Phelps and Emig, 153–90.

Heath, Shirley Brice. *Ways with Words: Language, Life, and Work in Communities and Classrooms.* London: Cambridge University Press, 1983.

Hekman, Susan J., ed. *Feminist Interpretations of Michel Foucault.* University Park: The Pennsylvania State University Press, 1996.

Hole, Judith, and Ellen Levine. *Rebirth of Feminism.* New York: Quadrangle Press, 1971.

hooks, bell. *Feminist Theory: From Margin to Center.* Boston: South End Press, 1984.

———. *Outlaw Culture: Resisting Representations.* New York: Routledge, 1994.

———. *Teaching to Transgress: Education as the Practice of Freedom.* New York: Routledge, 1994.

Jarratt, Susan C. "Introduction: As We Were Saying . . ." In Jarratt and Worsham, 1–18.

———. "Feminism and Composition: The Case for Conflict." In Harkin and Schilb, 105–23.

Jarratt, Susan C., and Lynn Worsham, eds. *Feminism and Composition Studies: In Other Words.* New York: MLA, 1998.

Johnson-Eilola, Johndan. *Nostalgic Angels: Rearticulating Hypertext Writing.* Norwood: Ablex, 1997.

———. "Reading and Writing in Hypertext: Vertigo and Euphoria." In Selfe and Hilligoss, 195–219.

Jones, Beverly, and Judith Brown. "Toward a Female Liberation Movement." In Tanner, 362–415.

Joreen [Jo Freeman]. "The Tyranny of Structurelessness." In Koedt, Levine, and Rapone, 285–99.

Joyce, Michael. "Siren Shapes: Exploratory and Constructive Hypertexts." *Academic Computing* 3 (1988): 10–15.

Kendall, Lori. "MUDer? I Hardly Know 'ER!: Adventures of a Feminist MUDder." In Cherny and Weise, 207–23.

Koedt, Anne, Ellen Levine, and Anita Rapone, eds. *Radical Feminism*. New York: Quadrangle Press, 1973.

Kraemer, Don. "No Exit: A Play of Literacy and Gender." *Journal of Advanced Composition* 10 (1990): 305–19.

Kreps, Bonnie. "Radical Feminism I." In Koedt, Levine, and Rapone, 234–39.

Landow, George, and Paul Delany, "Hypertext, Hypermedia, and Literary Studies: The State of the Art." In *Hypermedia and Literary Studies*, eds. Paul Delany and George Landow, 3–50. Cambridge: MIT Press, 1991.

Langstraat, Lisa R. "'Hypermasculinity' in Cultural Studies and Composition: Mapping a Feminist Response." *Composition Forum* 7 (1996): 1–16.

LeCourt, Donna, and Luann Barnes. "Writing Multiplicity: Hypertext and Feminist Textual Politics." *Computers and Composition* 16 (1999): 55–71.

Lorde, Audre. "The Master's Tools Will Never Dismantle the Master's House." *Sister Outsider: Essays and Speeches by Audre Lorde*. 110–113. Freedom: Crossing Press, 1984.

Lovibond, Sabina. "Feminism and Postmodernism." In *Postmodernism: A Reader*, ed. Thomas Docherty, 390–414. New York: Columbia University Press, 1993.

Luke, Carmen. "Feminist Politics in Radical Pedagogy." In Luke and Gore, 25–53.

Luke, Carmen, and Jennifer Gore, eds. *Feminisms and Critical Pedagogy*. New York: Routledge, 1992.

Lunsford, Andrea, Rebecca Rickly, Michael Salvo, and Susan West. "What Matters Who Writes? What Matters Who Responds? Issues of Ownership in the Writing Classroom." *Kairos* 1.1 (1996) [cited 25 June 2003]. Available from World Wide Web: <http://english.ttu.edu/kairos/1.1/features/lunsford/title.html> (25 June 2003).

Lunsford, Andrea A., Helene Moglen, and James Slevin, eds. *The Right to Literacy*. New York: MLA, 1990.

Malinowitz, Harriet. "A Feminist Critique of Writing in the Disciplines." In Jarratt and Worsham, 291–312.

Mattingly, Carol. "Valuing the Personal: Feminist Concerns for the Writing Classroom." In *Gender and Academe: Feminist Pedagogy and Politics,* eds. Sara Munson Deats and Lagretta Tallent Lenker, 153–66. Lanham: Rowman & Littlefield, 1994.

Miller, Susan. "The Feminization of Composition." In Bullock and Trimbur, 39–53.

———. *Rescuing the Subject: A Critical Introduction to Rhetoric and the Writer.* Carbondale: Southern Illinois University Press, 1989.

———. *Textual Carnivals: The Politics of Composition.* Carbondale: Southern Illinois University Press, 1990.

———. "Writing Theory::Theory Writing." In *Methods and Methodologies in Composition Research,* ed. Gesa E. Kirsch and Patricia A. Sullivan, 62–83. Carbondale: Southern Illinois University Press, 1992.

Millett, Kate. *Sexual Politics.* New York: Avon, 1971.

———. "Sexual Politics: A Manifesto for Revolution." In Koedt, Levine, and Rapone, 365–67.

Mitchell, Juliet. "Women: The Longest Revolution." In Schneir, 201–03.

Morgan, Robin. *Going Too Far: The Personal Chronicle of a Feminist.* New York: Random House, 1977.

———, ed. *Sisterhood is Powerful: An Anthology of Writings from the Women's Liberation Movement.* New York: Random, 1970.

Moulthrop, Stuart, and Nancy Kaplan. "They Became What They Beheld: The Futility of Resistance in the Space of Electronic Writing." In Selfe and Hilligoss, 220–37.

New York Radical Feminists. "Politics of the Ego: A Manifesto for N.Y. Radical Feminists." In Koedt, Levine, and Rapone, 379–83.

Nguyen, Mimi. *Exoticize My Fist!* [Cited 20 June 2003]. Available from World Wide Web: <http://members.aol.com/Critchicks>.

———. "Original Statement." *Exoticize My Fist!* September 1997 [cited 20 June 2003]. <http://members. aol.com/Critchicks/original.html>.

Norton, Eleanor Holmes. "For Sadie and Maude." In Morgan, *Sisterhood,* 397–404.

"Online Entertainment." *Cybergrrl, Inc.* 2000 [cited 13 March 2002]. Available from World Wide Web: <http://www.cgim.com/entertain.html>.

"Perfect Woman Rant." *GiRLRiGHtS.* 1996 [cited 18 September 1998]. Available from World Wide Web: <http://www.mmotion.com/grrrl/rants/perfect_woman.html>.

Phelps, Louise Wetherbee. "Becoming a Warrior: Lessons of the Feminist Workplace." In Phelps and Emig, *Feminine,* 289–39.

Phelps, Louise Wetherbee, and Janet Emig. "Editors' Reflections: Vision and Interpretation." In Phelps and Emig, *Feminine,* 407–25.

———, eds. *Feminine Principles and Women's Experience in American Composition and Rhetoric.* Pittsburgh: University of Pittsburgh Press, 1995.

Redstockings. "Redstockings Manifesto." In Schneir, 125–29.

Reid, Coletta, and Charlotte Bunch. "Revolution Begins at Home." In Bunch and Myron, 70–81.

Reynolds, Nedra. "Interrupting Our Way to Agency: Feminist Cultural Studies and Composition." In Jarratt and Worsham, 58–73.

Rhodes, Jacqueline. "'Substantive and Feminist Girlie Action': Women Online." *College Composition and Communication* 54 (2002): 116–42. Copyright 2002 by the National Council of Teachers of English. Reprinted with permission.

Ritchie, Joy. "Confronting the 'Essential' Problem: Reconnecting Feminist Theory and Pedagogy." *Journal of Advanced Composition* 10 (1990): 249–71.

Ritchie, Joy, and Kate Ronald. "Riding Long Coattails, Subverting Tradition: The Tricky Business of Feminists Teaching Rhetoric(s)." In Jarratt and Worsham, 217–38.

Royster, Jacqueline Jones. *Traces in a Stream: Literacy and Social Change Among African-American Women.* Pittsburgh: University of Pittsburgh Press, 2000.

Sarachild, Kathie. "Feminist Consciousness Raising and 'Organizing': Outline Prepared for a Lake Villa Workshop, November, 1968." In Tanner, 154–57.

Schell, Eileen E. "The Costs of Caring: 'Feminism' and Contingent Women Workers in Composition Studies." In Jarratt and Worsham, 74–93.

Schilb, John. *Between the Lines: Relating Composition Theory and Literary Theory.* Portsmouth: Boynton/Cook-Heinemann, 1996.

Schneir, Miriam, ed. *Feminism in Our Time: The Essential Writings, World War II to the Present*. New York: Vintage-Random House, 1994.

Selfe, Cynthia L. "Technology in the English Classroom: Computers through the Lens of Feminist Theory." In Handa, 118–39.

Selfe, Cynthia L., and Susan Hilligoss, eds. *Literacy and Computers: The Complications of Teaching and Learning with Technology*. New York: MLA, 1994.

Smithson, Isaiah, and Nancy Ruff, eds. *English Studies/Culture Studies*. Urbana: University of Illinois Press, 1994.

Solanas, Valerie. *SCUM Manifesto*. 1967. San Francisco: AK, 1996.

Southern Female Rights Union. "Southern Female Rights Union Program for Female Liberation." In Tanner, 112–15.

Stanger, Carol A. "The Sexual Politics of the One-To-One Tutorial Approach and Collaborative Learning." In Caywood and Overing, 31–44.

"Statement of Purpose." *Feminista!* 3.1. 1998 [cited 20 June 2003]. Available from World Wide Web: <http://www.feminista.com/v3n1/from-the-editor.html# purpose>.

Susan, Barbara. "About My Consciousness Raising." In Tanner, 238–43.

SWLAB Moderators. "The soc.women.lesbian-and-bi Moderation Policy." 14 November 2000 [cited 25 June 2003]. Available from World Wide Web: <http: //www.panix.com/~swlab-m/modpolicy.html>.

Tanner, Leslie B., ed. *Voices from Women's Liberation*. New York: Signet, 1971.

The 3rd WWWave: Feminism for a New Millennium. N. dat. [cited 20 June 2003]. Available from World Wide Web: <http://www.io.com/~wwwave/>.

Thompson, Sandye. "Speaking of the MOOn: Textual Realities and the Body Electric." *Kairos* 2.2 (Fall 1997) [cited 20 June 2003]. Available from World Wide Web: <http://english.ttu.edu/kairos/2.2/coverweb/sandye/tunnel1.html>.

Todd, Sharon. "Psychoanalytic Questions, Pedagogical Possibilities, and Authority: Encountering the 'And'." In Giroux and Shannon, 67–78.

Tong, Rosemarie. *Feminist Thought: A More Comprehensive Introduction*. 2nd ed. Boulder: Westview Press, 1998.

Wahlstrom, Billie J. "Communication and Technology: Defining a Feminist Presence in Research and Practice." In Selfe and Hilligoss, 171–85.

Weathers, Mary Ann. "An Argument for Black Women's Revolution As a Revolutionary Force." In Tanner, 303–07.

Worsham, Lynn. "After Words: A Choice of Words Remains." In Jarratt and Worsham, 329–56.

———. Guest lecture. University of South Florida, Tampa. 24 January 1997.

———. "Writing against Writing: The Predicament of *Ecriture Féminine* in Composition Studies." In Harkin and Schilb, 82–104.

Index